Joost

Joost

The Man in the Mirror

David Gemmell

Published by Zebra Press
an imprint of Random House Struik (Pty) Ltd
Reg. No. 1966/003153/07
80 McKenzie Street, Cape Town, 8001
PO Box 1144, Cape Town, 8000 South Africa

www.zebrapress.co.za

First published 2009

1 3 5 7 9 10 8 6 4 2

Publication © Zebra Press 2009
Text © David Gemmell and Joost van der Westhuizen 2009

Cover photograph © Gallo Images/Waldo Swiegers

Lyrics from 'Man in the Mirror' by Michael Jackson,
written by Siedah Garrett and Glen Ballard,
reproduced with permission of MCA and David Gresham Music

'The Guy in the Glass' © Dale Wimbrow 1934,
reproduced with permission of Peter Dale Wimbrow Jr.

PUBLISHER: Marlene Fryer
MANAGING EDITOR: Robert Plummer
EDITOR: Ronel Richter-Herbert
PROOFREADER: Beth Housdon
COVER AND TEXT DESIGNER: Natascha Adendorff-Olivier
TYPESETTER: Monique van den Berg
PRODUCTION MANAGER: Valerie Kömmer

Set in 11.5 pt on 15 pt Adobe Garamond

Printed and bound by CTP Book Printers, Cape

ISBN 978 1 77022 073 7

ISO 12647 compliant

To Jordan and Kylie

I'm Gonna Make A Change,
For Once In My Life
It's Gonna Feel Real Good,
Gonna Make A Difference
Gonna Make It Right...
  – Michael Jackson, 'Man in the Mirror'

Contents

Acknowledgements

Thank you to God, who has been very patient with me; to Amor for letting me know who I am and for saving my life; and hugs and kisses to my children Jordan and Kylie, my purpose in life. Thank you also to my long-suffering parents Gustav and Mariana; to my brothers Pieter and Gustav for always being there for me; to Amor's parents Dario and Delyse, and the rest of the Vittone family, for putting up with me; to all the people who support me regardless; to the life-support paramedics from Life Hospital; to Sunninghill Hospital; to Jenny, Bridget, Mario and Neville; and to my potential FEB (Future Ex-Buddy) Gemmell.

Joost Heystek van der Westhuizen
September 2009

More acknowledgements

I've always wondered why Oscar winners have such long lists of people to thank. Without for a second equating myself to a film star, I think I now know why. When I consider all the people who influenced me and assisted me in completing this book, I am astonished at just how many were required for me to do it all on my own.

Thank you to Martin Luitingh, who set the ball rolling; to the spectacularly competent and uncannily prescient Jenny Valsecchi; to my fiancée Dr Kym Morton for her indefatigable optimism, input and support; to Andy Rice, my constantly accessible, sagacious sounding board; to Justice Edwin Cameron and John Robbie for not letting me take the easy way out; to Richard Behrmann for, as always, being forthright; to the exceedingly generous Mike Barnes for letting us use his shack; to Nora for all the cups of coffee; to Bridget van Oerle for crying when she read the ending; to Annemarie van Wyk for the pivotal contact; to Zebra Press, particularly Robert Plummer and Ronel Richter-Herbert, for so unpatronisingly holding my hand; and to Jamie, Goosie and GJ for being perfect children (well, almost ...).

Lastly, thank you to Joost – without you, we had nothing.

David Gemmell
September 2009

Introduction

I don't believe this book needs an introduction. Hopefully it just says what it has to say. However, I would like to take this opportunity to make a request of my current NBF (New Best Friend):

The Shack
24 July 2009

Dear Joost

Despite the indescribably long hours spent writing (mine); despite the panic attacks (mine); despite the near-death experience (yours); despite the countless sleepless nights (ours); despite the soul-searching (everybody's); despite the nightmares (mine); despite the fear (yours); despite the emotional roller coaster we thought we would never get off (ours); despite the lack of faith in what we were doing (everybody else's); despite the pressure to complete this book (mine); despite the unenviable decisions made (yours); and despite the interminable hours I spent waiting for you to come to 'work' (mine), I have thoroughly enjoyed the experience.

If you ever want to do a sequel (to the book ...), I hope you will consider letting me write it for you.

Yours sincerely
David Gemmell

1

Writing Joost's book I

At the beginning of 2009, I contacted my mate Martin Luitingh in Australia. In a previous life, he and I had run the Comrades Marathon together, successfully paddled the Duzi Canoe Marathon and tried to annihilate each other in a bar fight at the Old Edwardian Club in Houghton.

He got the better of that particular battle when, by the simple expedient of cracking me above the left eye with an unopened bottle of beer, he laid me out cold. I don't bear grudges. I recall phoning him the next morning from the Johannesburg General Hospital and apologising for making him so angry.

Martin is an advocate, and when one of his colleagues made a pass at his wife, he decided he should raise his kids in a safer environment and moved to Australia. Regrettably, I lost touch with him.

At the beginning of this year, I idly thought it might be fun to find out what had happened to my erstwhile sparring mate. Even though it had been close on fifteen years since we last connected, I soon caught up with his life, and he mine. When he discovered that I had begun a belated career as a freelance writer and was doing sports interviews for the Weekender newspaper, Martin suggested I get hold of Joost van der Westhuizen's manager, Jenny Valsecchi.

Nothing like taking the direct route.

Given the possibility of an interview with the famous former Springbok scrumhalf (fast becoming infamous due to his uncanny resemblance to an individual caught nude on camera with a lady in a pink thong while allegedly inhaling quantities of white powder), I made immediate contact.

Jenny initially didn't think Joost would be interested in talking

1

to me, as his recently appointed press agent, Bridget van Oerle, had just stopped him talking to the media. I told Jenny it was high time someone reminded the public what a rugby legend Joost was; that he had been inducted into the Rugby Hall of Fame in the UK, etc., etc. And, I argued, 'He needs good press. I'll get it for him ...' I further allayed her scepticism by saying he could read the interview before it went to print.

Finally she yielded and gave me his number. I think she just wanted to shut me up.

Mind you, given the string of negative and, in some instances, downright abusive articles that were cropping up all over the place – particularly in Rapport, heat *and* Huisgenoot, *my request must have been an appealing distraction.*

When you meet Joost for the first time, you immediately understand why he generates so much public interest. Over six feet tall, he has a presence that, until you get used to him, is positively menacing. He is very good-looking in a slightly Germanic way, and his legendary 1000-mile, laser-like stare makes you feel as if he's continually studying the inside of your skull. His voice sounds as if he's swallowed one of those absurd voice-distortion gizmos you sometimes see in TV detective dramas – just better and more seductive.

He also seems to be utterly guileless.

The interview was interesting. I opened by saying that I had to ask him a couple of questions about his troubles, or else the piece would have no validity and come across as a whitewash. He had no problem with that. He is surprisingly receptive when he agrees, and downright terrifying when he disagrees.

The interview began thus:

DG: Suddenly you are appearing in the popular press, for all the wrong reasons. Normal people don't find themselves in these situations – what's really going on?

JvdW: I think somewhere in the past I have done something very wrong to somebody. I get attacked business-wise;

in my private life; in my individual life; and it's been going on for three years now. Whatever I do, I seem to get blocked and slammed. But I think we are getting to the bottom of it.

DG: **Is that you in the video?** *(I didn't add, but it was obviously implied, 'rolling around naked with the lady in the pink thong, snorting white powder?') His answer was unexpected. He looked me in the eyes with that terrifyingly reproachful, piercing stare and said:*

JvdW: Well, it's quite simple – I looked at the video and I can tell you now it isn't me.

DG: **Wrong answer. If it wasn't you in the video, you wouldn't have had to watch it. Let's start again.**

JvdW: Wait – before you do. If you were accused of being in something like [the video], wouldn't you have any interest, even maybe just to see how much the person resembled you? So I disagree that I didn't have to watch it once. *(As expected, he is certainly no pushover.)*

DG: **Okay, I take your point, but there is a simpler answer. Is that you in the video?** *(This time I didn't imply anything ...)*

JvdW: No.

The interesting aspect of his apparently incriminating first reply was that he is either a consummate actor, or he was sincerely trying to give me a definitive answer. He didn't blink as he answered; he didn't scratch his nose, pull his ear or do anything that could in any way be construed as a sign of someone not telling the truth. Another point in his favour, I reminded myself, was that he is Afrikaans – he speaks very good English, but it is his second language.

We duly completed the interview. As agreed, I let him read the piece and, with his approval, it was published in The Weekender *on 21 March 2009.*

A couple of days afterwards, Joost called to thank me. He said he was surprised to find that nothing had been altered and that the final copy was exactly as we had agreed. I was surprised that he was surprised.

About two weeks later, Joost again contacted me. He asked if I would be interested in writing a book with him. It was a bit like Madonna phoning and offering me a private show. Well, not quite, but you know what I mean.

I had, however, to temper the enthusiastic, gushing acceptance that welled up inside of me. Because, in my research on Joost for the sports interview, I'd discovered that Edward Griffiths had already written his biography (up until 1998): Joost: For Love and Money.

As if I was continually being inundated with requests to write books about legendary scrumhalves, I indifferently inquired why he would want another book so soon after Ed's.

His response was that, since 1998, a great deal had happened in his life that needed exposing – he thought a book would be the best way to go about it. I mentioned that if he was looking for someone to whitewash his indiscretions – an obviously unspoken allusion to 'the video' – then I wasn't his man.

'No,' Joost said. 'I will tell you stuff that will make your eyes water. With regard to the video – that will be in the last chapter, and it is going to blow everyone's socks off.'

I have a penchant for having my socks blown off, so of course I was in.

'Okay, I'll do it,' I said. 'But don't tell me what is in the last chapter, or I might have to give up the project before we've even started.'

He just laughed.

At the back of my mind I thought that no matter what his involvement in the scandal – wrong or right, innocent or guilty – by the time we got to write the last chapter, events would have overtaken the situation and the last few pages would write themselves. By then it would either have been conclusively proven who it was in the video, or Joost would have confessed. Either way, I was covered.

2

1998 Currie Cup

'*Fok, manne!*' screamed Joost. '*Wat gaan aan?*'

Against the run of play, the Natal Sharks fullback, André Joubert, had broken through a half-hearted Bulls tackle and scored a try.

Joost scowled at his team. In a voice that could freeze fire, he barked, '*Kom manne, kom*! This is *our* turn. This is *our* Currie Cup.'

Alas, it seemed this was not to be. Moments after the second-half kick-off, a perfectly timed pass from Natal scrumhalf Kevin Putt to André Joubert, cutting in on the blind side, sent the Rolls-Royce of fullbacks gliding over for his second try.

Again the Bulls players disconsolately gathered beneath their goalposts on the sunny Saturday afternoon. Studiously avoiding their captain's penetrating stare and wishing they were somewhere else, they waited for Natal wing Gavin Lawless to take the conversion.

A successful kick would stretch the Natal Sharks' lead in this semi-final of the 1998 Currie Cup competition to 14 points. Lawless carefully placed the ball on the Day-Glo kicking tee, quaintly delivered by a miniature radio-controlled Jeep. All the while the Loftus faithful, in loyal support of the Blue Bulls' fading chances of finally becoming Currie Cup champions again, heaped invective on his perspiring head.

But the ref's whistle signalled continued bad news for the light-blue-clad masses as the ball sailed dead centre through the uprights.

At the northern end of the field, the massive screen displayed Sharks 17, Bulls 3.

'Damn it!' thought Joost. 'This is our Currie Cup, not bloody Natal's.'

On his bench alongside the touchline, below the packed main stand, Blue Bulls coach Eugene van Wyk despaired. After so many months of blood, sweat and tears, how could this be happening? What more did the rugby gods want? (Given the emotion at that moment, he probably didn't reflect on why those obviously fickle gods should favour the Blue Bulls' efforts and not Natal's.)

'Listen to the crowd … Listen!' As Joost yelled at his men, he emphasised his remarks with an exaggerated sweep of his arm. Then, doing his best to contain himself, he looked his players in the eye and, just loud enough to be heard over the roar of the heaving stadium, calmly said, 'Those people have supported us through thick and thin. Now it's our turn to do something good for them. To do something we can feel proud of. Stop worrying about whether we are going to win or not; let's just play with pride and guts. Then, when we go home, we can still look at ourselves in the mirror.'

Eugene van Wyk had just given up on questioning the motives of the dithering rugby gods when, in typically opportunistic play by Van der Westhuizen, the Bulls' scrumhalf and captain, in a moment of sheer rugby brilliance, put the blind-side flanker through for a try.

It happened when a ferocious tackle on Lawless by Franco Smith saw the ball squirt free, whereupon Joost immediately hacked it forward. Predator-like, the tall scrumhalf sidestepped and jinked his way through a phalanx of wrong-footed Sharks players, swooped on the loose ball and, despite the desperate attentions of the giant Natal and Springbok lock Mark Andrews, popped it up for flank Nicky van der Walt to burst through, punch the air with his fist and cross the line for a critically needed five points.

But the move resulted in more than just points. It sparked a rearguard action in the Bulls that any elite fighting unit would be proud of. With rediscovered gusto, the hitherto listless men in blue tore into the Sharks like epileptic madmen. It was now *their* ball, and they were not going to let Natal play with it; after all, they wanted to be able to face themselves in the mirror when they got home …

When Joost's increasingly rampant *manne* were awarded a penalty try after Grant Esterhuizen was tripped on his way to the ball in the in-goal area, coach Eugene van Wyk silently revised his opinion of the rugby deities. On the field, Joost raised his clenched fists and roared with delight.

The 48 000 Bulls fans lapped up every minute as they watched the greatest fightback in their team's history.

When the final whistle was blown, the scoreboard read Sharks 17, Bulls 31. An improbable victory for Joost's *manne*, but one they would gladly take. Their place in the 1998 Currie Cup final was secure.

The Currie Cup

The Absa Currie Cup is the premier domestic rugby competition in South Africa. In 1891, when a British Isles team arrived in the country – the first overseas players to tour South Africa – they brought with them a striking, valuable golden cup. It had been given to the visiting squad by Sir Donald Currie, owner of the Union-Castle Line, the shipping company that had transported the team to the southern tip of Africa. Sir Donald was clear with his instructions – they were to hand this trophy over to the first side to beat them. As it transpired, the visitors were unbeaten, but the side that lost by the least, Griqualand West, became the first-ever holders of the Currie Cup. Griqualand donated the trophy to the rugby board, and it subsequently became the prize for the Currie Cup competition. In 1892, the inaugural Currie Cup tournament was held, with Western Province the first winners. To this day, the trophy remains the holy grail of South African rugby.

'en days later, barely recovered from their heroic exploits
...u-final, Joost's *manne* descended from the team bus and
made their way through the players' entrance of the formidable
concrete rugby cathedral that is Loftus Versfeld. The final of
the 1998 Currie Cup against Western Province was about to be
decided.

In the previous day's edition of *Business Day*, Pieter Kruger
had opined as follows:

> I believe the skilful Western Province outfit will beat the Blue
> Bulls tomorrow afternoon. Western Province have too much
> class, individual talent, big-match temperament and [too
> many] match breakers in the likes of Percy Montgomery,
> Breyton Paulse, Pieter Rossouw, Robbie Fleck, Christian
> Stewart, Toks van der Linde, Selborne Boome and Bobby
> Skinstad (all Springboks) and will retain the cup.

It seems that local boy Conrad Breytenbach hadn't read that
edition of *Business Day* and thus didn't know that the Bulls were
expected to lose. After just 90 seconds, he charged up the blind-
side wing and burst through to score to the left of the posts: Bulls
7-Western Province 0.

For the rest of the first half, the Bulls forwards took charge
of the set pieces. They also retained better possession in the loose
than their star-studded opposition. The men in blue had come
into the game with a point to prove against a Western Province
pack that contained three new Springboks in Johnny Trystman,
Selborne Boome and Corné Krige – and prove it they did.

The next day, writing in the *Sunday Times*, eminent sports
writer Dan Retief said the following:

> Bulls skipper Joost van der Westhuizen was a smouldering
> and unpredictable presence for most of the match with his
> ability to pressure the inside backs of the opposition, but it
> was fitting that a cat-like thrust [by Joost] resulted in what
> turned out to be the winning try.

Shortly before the restart, Van Zyl grubbered a ball straight to Bulls fullback Hannes Venter, who passed in-field to Van der Westhuizen. Pure instinct took over as the man playing in his first final spotted that Province was vulnerable on their left flank. He ran clear before passing to André Snyman, who in turn fed the enormous young Wim Meyer, who had replaced Breytenbach.

Meyer stepped inside the attempted tackles of Skinstad and Christian Stewart and then swung outside Breyton Paulse to score a try that will be preserved as one of the chosen few in the annals of Bulls history.

Western Province hung in bravely, but when Percy Montgomery had to leave the field with a torn hamstring, robbing them of attacking flair and a reliable goal-kicker, it seemed the vacillating rugby gods had determined that it was coach Eugene van Wyk's team's turn to hold the cup aloft – again. Van Wyk had coached the Bulls when they last won the golden trophy, in 1991. (In typical rugby management contortions, he had been subsequently fired, but later rehired.)

Eighty minutes after the game had begun in such dramatic fashion, exhausted but jubilant, the Bulls emerged from a series of seemingly never-ending tackles, rucks and mauls as 1998 Currie Cup champions. Western Province was gutted. With their 10 Springboks, they had been the overwhelming favourites, but in the end they had simply underwhelmed (although, to be fair, only just). They lost 20-24.

Thus, after six years of trying and a litany of disappointments, Joost van der Westhuizen won his first Currie Cup. After the match, the press quoted him as saying, 'This feels better than winning the World Cup', a remark that aroused indignation in the upper echelons of South African rugby – not for the first or last time would the press cause ructions in Joost's life.

'Wasn't winning the Rugby World Cup in 1995 the greatest

South African rugby achievement ever?' asked the leading lights of South African rugby administration, as if they themselves had won the Webb Ellis Trophy.

'Of course winning the World Cup against all the rugby-playing nations of the world was South African rugby's greatest achievement,' says Joost. 'The World Cup was always going to be the more prestigious event to win. But for six years I had been trying, without success, to win a Currie Cup.'

When he did eventually land the elusive prize, his success represented the culmination of years of hard grind. Conversely, in his mind, the World Cup equated to only six months of direct effort and, as he notes, 'I didn't have to first lose six [World Cups] along the way before I got my hands on my first one.'

At the beginning of 1998, all that had been missing from the plethora of rugby goals Joost had set and achieved was winning the Currie Cup. As he, his proud *manne* and the trophy did a weary lap of honour through the deepening shadows of Loftus Versfeld Stadium and wallowed in the adoring crowd's tumultuous praise, he knew he would set new targets, because that was his way. He just wasn't going to be bothering with them much that night.

From an early age, rugby had been Joost's life. In 1977, he was five years old when he started school, and he wanted to play the game even then. But according to school rules, he had to wait until he was six years old before he would be allowed to play. Undeterred, he kept nagging until his coach, Johan Botha, relented and gave him a game.

'At one stage they played me on the wing, but I never got the ball. They tried me as a prop and a flank, but there was always not enough ball for me. I then decided I wanted to play scrum-half, because they got lots of ball. Weird to think how, when it came to rugby, although I was only five or six years old, I knew exactly what I wanted. I wanted the bloody ball,' Joost says with an infectious laugh.

So, as a barefoot boy at Laerskool Derdepoort, in a poor area on the eastern side of Pretoria, he had already showed glimmers of the extraordinarily unyielding purpose he would later display on rugby fields around the world – much to his opposition's despair.

'Interestingly,' recalls Joost, 'our coach, Johan, used to call us his "little Springboks". Maybe that is where the seed was planted in me.' His budding desire to excel at the game was fuelled by frequent trips to Loftus Versfeld to watch the Bulls and see legends like Thys Lourens and Naas Botha in action. After the games, he would run onto the field to touch his heroes.

'From then on, it was what I wanted to do. Rugby was a way for me to express myself. Other kids would jump on their bikes or run or whatever. All I wanted to do was play rugby.'

He recalls how, in high school, he was late for maths class because he had been playing touch rugby. The teacher, Miss Kriel, made him sit in the front of the class with some of his partners in crime. 'You rugby players,' she lectured, 'will never make a living out of rugby – so better you start learning.'

Ten years later, at a class reunion, Miss Kriel asked Joost for an autograph for her son. 'I said, "No, hold on, Miss Kriel. Remember what you told me about rugby? First apologise, then I will sign for your boy."' He smiles as he recalls the look on her face.

The Miss Kriel story reminds Joost of the first autograph he ever gave. Just before his debut game for the Bulls, all the players walked out onto the practice field and some of them started signing autographs for the public. 'One or two of us just stood around – no one knew who we were. And then a father brought his son over to me and said, "Please will you sign my son's rugby ball?" Of course, I said – I was surprisingly nervous.'

The father then turned to his son and asked him if he knew who Joost was. The little guy shook his head. 'He is the new scrum-half for Northern Transvaal,' the father explained.

'I'd always wanted to be famous, so I thought, "Here's my chance!" And I remember that I signed my whole name, with all the vowels and using every letter. I actually felt quite silly, not "real" at all, like I was acting a part. Later my signature became no vowels and as short and quick as possible.' He laughs. 'The funny thing is, I saw the autograph again last year. The guy found me at some function and showed it to me.'

Joost couldn't believe his eyes – his old autograph was typical high-school, immature, 'polite' writing. 'He asked me to sign the ball again. My new signature looked nothing like the original.

'Another incident I remember took place in 1992, when I played for Northern Transvaal. Adriaan Richter, the captain, said to me: "Enjoy every minute of your career, because before you blink it's going to be over." I just looked at him and said, "Yeah, right. I've got *ten years* left," and suddenly here we sit and it's all over – long ago.

'Interestingly, my grandfather played for the Springbok Vlakte, a team named after the area in which they played. Tongue-in-cheek, they called themselves "the Springboks". So maybe I also got some of his genes,' says Joost, smiling. 'The other day my mother dug out a picture of me wearing my junior Springbok jersey, standing next to my grandfather. All I could see when she showed it to me was my stupid hairstyle.'

In the age groups, Joost always played in the A sides. He played Craven Week in 1988; won the schools' Administrators Cup at Loftus while Under-15; played Under-19 and Under-20 for Northern Transvaal; and then, in 1992, started with the senior team.

Astonishingly, Joost mentions that, apart from the Administrators Cup, the first 'big cup' he won was the World Cup in 1995. 'It might be a useless fact, but I have never lost a final. When I was in a final, I won it.'

So, as far as rugby was concerned, Joost always knew what he wanted and where he was headed. The way forward for the rest of his life was more obscure, but infinitely less important to the unsophisticated youth.

3

Writing Joost's book II

We discuss starting the book with a summary of his rugby career up to 1998 (already dealt with in detail in Edward Griffiths' book), and then covering his career in more depth from 1999 until his retirement in 2003. Later we will attack, so to speak, his personal life.

'The first thing we need to do,' I say, 'is to write a synopsis of what we are planning with the book. A publisher will want to know what they're getting and we'll know where we're going.'

We bounce around various ideas and topics, discussing and then listing the contentious events in his life that might be of interest to the reader. We are trying to plan events chronologically, and when we get to the year 2007, Joost suddenly looks up and says, 'That's when I told my dad and two brothers to get out of my life – although I wasn't that polite.'

'Oh,' I say. 'Given all your battles with virtually everyone you've ever met, is there anybody you haven't told to get stuffed?'

He looks at me and, with a mirthless grin, says, 'You.'

Oh dear ...

Over the next few days, I work diligently on the synopsis. Fully aware that it is fundamentally the one chance we have of convincing a publisher that we have a product they should buy, I keep asking myself: 'What is there about Joost that people would want to read?'

The problem is, I come up with answers I don't think Joost will want to hear. However, I assume that Joost is quite media savvy, and given the feeding frenzy that has been going on in the gutter press about what has become known as 'Joostgate', he has to have a clue.

I pull up a chair at our by-now regular meeting spot, Frappé in Dainfern Valley Centre, greet the waiting Joost and ask if he wants *breakfast. He smiles at me as if to say, 'You're buying time – you're not sure about your bloody synopsis.'*

Remarkably astute, because although he doesn't actually say anything, I know this is what he is thinking, and he is spot on. I am petrified. As I mentioned earlier, Joost has a menacing presence that no doubt caused huge apprehension in big, tough rugby players all over the world when he was running rampant on their fields. It therefore wasn't difficult for him to intimidate me.

Having placed orders for various permutations of scrambled and poached eggs, there is nothing more to do other than let him read what I have written.

Joost has a very disconcerting, expressionless way of reading. Until he hands back a document to you, sometimes accompanied by a guttural, 'Good,' you simply have no idea how he is going to react.

He reads through the one-and-a-half-page synopsis in silence and then glares at me. At least, it looks like a glare. His stare is so unsettling, I'm never quite sure if it is disapproving or not.

'It's a bit harsh.'

'I know,' I say. 'But you are aware of what we are trying to do and what people want to read. No one wants to read 400 bloody match reports in a row or detailed descriptions of every try you scored.'

He doesn't react, but simply carries on staring at me.

'They want to know why you broke the boom at Dainfern and what happened when you and Amor sued Loslyf *magazine. They want to know what makes you real, like them. They want to know about you and Amor. They love nothing more than to find out that famous people also have problems and sometimes behave badly. That people like you also have to go to the toilet, have to clean their teeth and need to eat food.'*

I purposefully leave out any mention of the video, suspecting that it might provoke something that could halt the project before it has even started. I take the document back from him. 'Okay, what would you like me to change?'

'Nothing – but it's still harsh.' He smiles and tucks into his four eggs scrambled; no toast.

4

Upbringing

'I was born into apartheid – I never agreed to it,' says Joost rather naively, echoing the sentiments of most of his generation. As not exactly profound yet telling evidence of his non-racial attitude – his 'colour blindness' from an early and formative age – he mentions the times he spent on his grandfather's farm during his school holidays. (In establishing his non-racial credentials, he omits to mention that he named his son Jordan, after the black basketball player Michael Jordan, who, as far as Joost is concerned, is the archetypal all-round superstar and most amazing sportsman the world has ever seen.)

The farm Hanover was about 30 kilometres east of Warmbaths in the then Northern Transvaal. The landscape was very flat, with nary a hill in sight. About 60 per cent of the land was cultivated, while the rest was typical bushveld. 'It was very neat and tidy,' says Joost. 'My grandfather always kept everything very ordered. It was a typical Afrikaner farm. He always seemed to be well prepared for the next season, whether it was ploughing, planting or reaping.'

His *oupa*, Joost Heystek Pretorius, farmed cattle and sheep and grew maize. Each time 'klein Joost' arrived at the farm, he would seek out his black mate Petrus, the son of farmhand Jackson, for, among other things, a game of *kleilat*.

The game involved tightly moulding a wad of wet clay onto the end of a poplar branch about 1.5 metres long and with the thickness of a light rod. Using a whiplash action, the gob of clay would then be lethally propelled at whatever enemy the children could conjure up. Given that the clay flew at the speed of light, with the same force as a hurled brick, and that the enemy inevitably comprised the other farm workers' kids or Joost's brothers, Gustav and Pieter, it was astonishing that no life-threatening injuries were ever sustained.

When not indulging in inter-pasture ballistic warfare, and if they could be found by Oupa Joost, the boys would be deployed to look after the animals. They used to help when the male calves were neutered.

'As young boys, we had so much fun with that. We would rugby-tackle the calves and hold them down so that the workers could snip them. We used to think we were real cowboys, having our own rodeos.'

It is obvious from his enthusiastic reminiscing that the farm days were an extremely happy part of Joost's life.

'I remember one time I grabbed a calf around the neck and I was pulling it down when I heard my brother shouting, "Watch out! Behind you, watch out!" The mother of the calf had got into the paddock and was charging at me. You have never seen anyone do low flying like I did to get away from her. I just flew through the bottom strands of the barbed-wire fence,' he laughs.

For 'klein Joost', the school holidays always raced past in a kaleidoscope of adventure, exploration, chores, wars and dreams of derring-do on the world's great rugby fields.

In those halcyon days, as they planted maize, the young white boy and his black companion would chat (in Afrikaans) about their hopes and dreams. In their simple world, apartheid didn't exist.

Growing up as he did in a typical Afrikaner family goes a long way in explaining the enigma that is Joost van der Westhuizen. His conservatism, his defiant nature, his arrogance and his toughness all stem from that basic fact. But just as his genealogy explains a lot, it leaves as much unclear.

Joost's inquiring mind, entrepreneurship, outspokenness and

forthright, liberal views are all at odds with his background. His parents are fantastically proud of him, but in many respects have no idea where he comes from.

As a child, his mother Mariana would wake him on a Sunday to go to church. Sometimes, preferring to sleep, he would ask, 'Why do I have to go?'

'*Sommer*,' she would reply.

'Why?' Joost would repeat.

'Because God says so,' would be her final word. To her it was simple. But her son wanted more.

'Older generations of Afrikaners don't like solutions that are complex, difficult or ambiguous. If you can't explain it in terms of good or bad, they don't want to know,' says Joost. 'That is why other nations and their cultures are inevitably viewed by Afrikaners as good or bad, friend or foe. There are no shades of grey.'

In the world in which his mother had been raised and which she and her husband, Gustav, were introducing to Joost, children either obeyed their parents or they were disciplined. In the Van der Westhuizen household, discipline normally took the form of a sound thrashing, administered by Gustav and his trouser belt. It was a thrashing that never hurt physically. 'It hurt up here,' says Joost, tapping the side of his head.

In his Afrikaner parents' world, observes Joost, you didn't question – you weren't allowed to. 'Not taking "no" for an answer from their conservative point of view was wrong and disrespectful.' According to Joost, he would rather have the truth unsweetened and properly explained – just what it was, nothing more. He wanted to be able to doubt, to experience, to think, to challenge and to criticise.

Apart from the diaspora and Namibia, Afrikaans is spoken only in South Africa. Afrikaners make up 59 per cent of South Africa's 4.3 million whites. But they are just 5.6 per cent of the overall population of 45 million. So they are a small, albeit influential, part of the whole.

The Afrikaners are descendants of 17th-century Dutch, German and French settlers who left their homelands, motivated by a restless desire to move on and make something of their lives. When their forefathers arrived on southern African soil, the convicts still hadn't reached Australia or the future Americans their new country, facts Afrikaners often quote as if they have a profound relevance to their own history, or imbue them with some indefinable vicarious merit.

Afrikaners see themselves as Africans – they know no other home, and the absolute majority have no intention of leaving South Africa. They resent being called settlers ... or Dutchmen, rock-spiders, planks, hairybacks, crunchies ...

Afrikaners are truly an unusual bunch. For various reasons, probably completely justifiable, from the time they arrived here, they fought. If they weren't battling the local inhabitants of wherever they settled, the Boers, as they were known, clashed with the British. And fighting was something they did particularly well. Tough and fearless, they were prepared to die for their beliefs, which, of course, made them a formidable enemy to face.

The following extract from *The Origins of the South African War 1899–1902* by Iain Smith is instructive:

The South African War of 1899–1902 was the most exten-sive, costly and humiliating war fought by Britain between the defeat of Napoleon in 1815 and the outbreak of the First World War in 1914. It involved over four times as many troops as the Crimean War and cost more than three times as much in money. On the eve of the War, the British gov-ernment estimated that a war in South Africa might cost 10 million pounds, require a maximum of 75,000 troops, might result in – at worst – a few hundred casualties, and be over within three or four months. The combined Afrikaner population, of what were then two of the world's smallest states, amounted to less than 250,000 with Boer forces fielding less than 45,000. In the event, the war cost some 230 million pounds, involved a total of 450,000 British and Empire troops, and resulted in the deaths of almost 22,000 combatants on the British side. (It lasted three years and the Boers lost 3,900 men on the battlefield.)

With religion, and some would say racism, indelibly imprinted in their cultural DNA, and with absolute faith in God and themselves, the Afrikaners took on all comers.

In a rugby context, this can be seen when the Springboks – still largely dominated by Afrikaners – kneel and pray before or after a game. It is a ritual they seem to follow more when the captain is Afrikaans and they are victorious. This scenario unfolded after the Springboks won the 1995 World Cup. At the end of the game, Springbok captain François Pienaar, also from an Afrikaans background, called his team around him on the field for a brief moment of prayer. Joost says that all they were doing was thanking the Lord for seeing them safely through the game.

Praying, according to him, was never about asking God to favour his team in a match, or about thanking God for a victory at the expense of the defeated – 'Especially when the defeated were New Zealand,' he laughs. (Although, after winning the Currie Cup at Loftus in 1998, Van der Westhuizen was quoted in the national press as saying he felt the outcome was 'the will of God. My young team were hungry to win – but they could not do so without God's help.')

Apart from their fighting and religion, what else is quintessentially Afrikaans? Crimplene or khaki? Biltong or boerewors? *Spook 'n diesel* or beer? Leon Schuster or De la Rey? Pik Botha or Naas Botha? *Koffie en beskuit* or *tee en melktert*? *Pap en vleis* or venison and *droeë perskes*? Sakkie-sakkie or disco? Rugby or *jukskei*?

As in every culture, contradictions exist, but there is hardly a thing that can be said about the Afrikaner where the reverse is not true. The same would appear to apply to Joost van der Westhuizen.

Joost is a proud man, but surprisingly humble when he watches and delights in his children at play. Once arrogant, born out of a lifetime of having been told he was the best, he is self-effacing when helping out the many charities he is able to assist from the hundreds who ask for his patronage. He is tough as nails, but as weak as a kitten when instructed by his wife, the gorgeous Amor. 'Her wish is my command,' he says, smiling. He is outspoken when he strongly opposes an issue and deceptively quiet when he agrees.

Beneath the surface of one of the world's legendary, tough and most complex rugby players lurks a beguiling humility that, intentionally or otherwise, he has largely succeeded in keeping to himself.

Conversely, the picture of him that regularly emerges from the pages of the national press (especially in the last few years) is more often than not unflattering; one of an arrogant, womanising social gadfly who provokes endless curiosity among the chattering classes. The fact that he is good-looking, famous, in perfect shape and apparently wealthy only fuels the rumours.

After school, Joost attended Pretoria University (Tuks, or Tukkies). He had actually wanted to go to the Teachers' Training College, but his headmaster at Hoërskool FH Odendaal, Fonnie van der Vyver, insisted Joost study hard in order to obtain a matric exemption, which would enable him to attend university. Van der Vyver told Joost he could always do a teaching diploma after he had a degree. 'Without me knowing it, he was putting me on the high road for my future career,' says Joost, who still has enormous respect and affection for his erstwhile mentor.

Compulsory national service had just been dropped, so Joost missed out on what had become a rite of passage for most white South African youths – a fact that might, to some degree, explain his support for the infamous Kamp Staaldraad (discussed later).

At Tuks, Joost did a Bachelor of Arts degree in Physical Education, and he reckons that those were three of the best years of his life.

During that period, in the early 1990s, he found himself playing rugby with his heroes: Naas Botha, Adriaan Richter, Jan Lock, Adolf Malan ... For the young Joost, it was surreal. 'I just went, *wow*! It's what I'd always dreamt of.'

Considering that Naas Botha started playing for the Northern Transvaal senior side when Joost was in Grade 1, it must have been a huge adjustment for the young player.

Smiling, Joost remembers an occasion when Bulls coach John Williams criticised various players after a particularly awful match. Williams had just torn strips off about five players, telling them how absolutely useless they had been, when he turned to Joost and said, 'Well, at least you had the crowd on their feet all night.'

Joost hardly had time to feel relieved before Williams continued, 'Yes, they spent the whole bloody game on their feet, trying to catch all the balls you kicked out on the full into the stands.'

But Joost was enjoying himself. 'Suddenly the whole world revolved around me. I was *the man*. It's a false sense of life, but you don't realise it. It's only when your career is over and you look back that you realise how silly it all was.'

And he used to drink a lot. 'The problem was, when you were at school, you lived with your parents and they were there to guide you. But once you got to university, you lived on your own. You met new friends and you got pissed, and you missed classes.'

Hardly the crime of the century, but something he feels is worth mentioning.

Then the rugby team became his family. 'So when they got drunk, I got drunk. What they said was right was what I said was right. Also, I was taught that if there was a problem in the team, we went and got pissed. When we got back, everything was sorted.' He adds, 'I believe that nowadays they only drink on a Saturday night.'

Then, looking marginally contrite, he continues, 'In fact, as recently as 2006, after commentating on a match for SuperSport at Loftus, I went down to the change rooms for a drink with the boys. I only got home at five o'clock the next morning. Amor was waiting for me, so I knew I was in trouble. But because of my past, I had all the backstops; I could get out of any sort of mess. Remember, I'd been through a divorce and other difficult situations before.'

Unwittingly, he had just exposed how the appeal of the drinking culture of the old days still had a grip on him, years after he had ostensibly withdrawn from it.

Amor sat him down and then brought him some coffee. Without raising her voice, she said, 'You've got a son up there,' pointing upstairs. 'You're beginning to show me that you don't care about him or me but only about yourself. You have to decide now whether you are in this marriage or not. Do this again, and Jordan and I walk.'

In that instant, Joost had an epiphany. He suddenly realised what he had been doing.

'Thousands of years ago, Jesus said, "Father, forgive them, for they know not what they do." Well, that no longer applied to me, because I suddenly knew what I was doing. I can almost track how my life changed from that very moment.'

While he was playing for the Bulls, Joost worked as a security guard. 'I had to work. That was when rugby was still amateur. After every game we would each get a little brown envelope with a few rand inside to cover our expenses, but it certainly wasn't money in any real sense of the word.'

When asked how he squared his religion with his bad-boy years, Joost replies, 'The simple explanation is I forgot to listen from the first split second of an answer. Let me explain. If you ask yourself, "Should I be doing this?", usually your conscience immediately tells you whether you should or shouldn't be doing it. But if in the first split second you ignore what your conscience says, you just find excuses for doing what you want to do.'

He claims that one's conscience is actually the lessons learnt from one's parents. 'I always remember that scene in *The Lion King* when Simba sees his father's face in the water and it says, "Son, always remember who you are." That's the problem – you forget your upbringing and you forget who you are, and that's when the trouble starts in your life. That's what I call reality.'

5

Writing Joost's book III

Joost has given me a set of DVDs – Springbok Saga – as my home-work. I think he is getting gatvol of me asking blatantly ignorant questions. In his world, you remember every minute of every match – every tackle, every kick, every dummy and every try. You remember every stadium, every result, the name of every player on your team and, if he was any good, your opponent's.

I have, of course, noticed that a lot of what went on off the field seems to have been forgotten. With Joost it is very much a case of 'what goes on tour stays on tour'.

We are once again sitting at Frappé. The waitress wants to take our order. 'Are you having your three scrambled eggs again?' I ask.

'Four,' he says. 'It's always four – no toast.'

'I'll have two poached eggs with toast,' I say to the girl.

The order out of the way, I ask Joost for his copy of Ed Griffiths' book so that I can see what he wrote.

'I'll bring it tomorrow. Can you read Afrikaans? I don't have an English version.'

We chat. The waitress brings the food. Four eggs scrambled for Joost, and three, not two, poached eggs on toast for me.

'The waitress was listening to our conversation when I asked you if you were going to have three eggs, and for some reason that number stuck in her brain,' I say. He finds it very amusing. For someone who can be so forceful, he is intriguingly undemanding. I'm always the one who wants no 'sprinkles' on his cappuccino, or no raw onions in the salad, or more ice. He simply tolerates or ignores the little mishaps and sloppy service that seem endemic in local restaurants.

A new article has appeared in one of the scandal magazines alleging that Joost is broke.

'So are you?' I ask.

He laughs. 'If you look at the sponsorships they say I have lost, you will see that most of them expired over a year ago. With the economic crunch, most of them weren't renewed. But they weren't renewed for anyone, so it wasn't as if I was being singled out. Also, they say that I didn't pay my lawyer, with the result that she stopped working for me, and that's just bullshit. I might not be as wealthy as I once was, but with the economy the way it is I don't think anyone is. However, I am certainly not platsak. By the way,' he continues, laughing, 'when I leave, you must remind me to take some sugar sachets home ...'

'What about that book some female journalist is bringing out in which she says Amor used to hate it when you put away your underwear if it had holes in it?' I ask. 'She's obviously trying to make some connection between you and the video, where the guy apparently has holes in his underpants.'

'Dave, you've been to my house – does it look like I do the laundry or, for that matter, put it away? And do you think Amor always watches my laundry being put away and can see holes in piles of underpants? It is just such utter rubbish; I don't know how we are supposed to respond. It happens all the time – little articles keep appearing that are either rehashed rumours or just plain crap – but they keep coming.'

On the basis that obviously not everything can be false or made up (after all, I write for various publications, most of which are surprisingly rigorous in ensuring the veracity of what they publish), I am tempted to suggest that he doth protest too much. But more and more I am becoming convinced by his arguments. I hope, of course, that changing some, or all, of my beliefs will not in any way compromise having my socks blown off ...

But I sympathise with the Van der Westhuizens. Ever since Joost has become my NBF, I have grown more aware of how frequently the press have a crack at him and Amor. Conversely, I have also noticed a groundswell of sympathy for them from virtually everyone I talk to.

'Who cares if it is Joost in that video?'

'It's his life and it's got stuff-all to do with anyone.'

'What's with these people that they become so obsessed with celebrities' lives?'

'What has it to do with anyone else but them?'

'It just shows how shallow the lives are of those people who enjoy that stuff.'

'Why all the fuss? There have always been hookers and white lines in rugby ...'

'I never read that rubbish or buy those stupid magazines.'

But someone does. They sell thousands of copies to people who seem to delight in the couple's misfortunes. Even if the misfortunes are apocryphal.

Of course, it is not, as Joost would have me believe, just a South African (Afrikaner) phenomenon. It happens everywhere in the world.

By comparison with, for example, the Beckhams, Joost and Amor's media plight is simply a non-event. If David Beckham had scored with all the girls with whom he is alleged to have scored, or he and Victoria responded to every defamatory article that appeared, he wouldn't have any time to play football and she wouldn't have any time to diet.

So most, if not all of the stories about Beckham's wandering ways have to be nothing more than, as Joost so eloquently puts it, 'bullshit'.

Going back to the nascent support for Joost I am discovering: it's fascinating how even these supporters of Joost's right to privacy still want to know if I think it is him in the video.

'Read the book,' I say, 'and all will be revealed. Your socks will be blown off.'

6

Joost the rugby star

With 38 tries in 89 test matches, Joost van der Westhuizen is the highest try-scoring South African player ever to don the green-and-gold jersey. He is also the most prolific try-scoring test scrumhalf of all time.

Interview with Joost van der Westhuizen

It appears no one did stop you. You scored 38 tries for South Africa, the most tries ever scored by a Springbok, and you have scored the most test tries by a scrumhalf.
It's all about peripheral vision; about understanding your position and being a team player. I never did it for myself – I did it for the team.

When you look back, do you have a favourite [try]?
Yes, at the end of 1995 we toured the UK. In the test against England at Twickenham, I got the ball from a prop and I broke. I had to jink and jive; kick; push away tacklers; dodge players; chip the ball – it was like a dog competition for humans. I had to use most of my skills to score it.

The Weekender, 21–22 March 2009

An integral part of the 1995 Rugby World Cup–winning team, Joost was in the victorious 1998 Tri-Nations squad and captain of the Springboks in the 1999 World Cup. They achieved third place in that tournament after being thwarted in the dying minutes of the semi-finals by a Stephen Larkham drop goal for Australia. In the playoff, the Springboks beat New Zealand 22-18. That same year Joost captained the Blue Bulls to win the Currie Cup, and in 2007 he was inducted into the International Rugby Hall of Fame in England.

He is also the only Springbok to captain his country in both the Sevens and the 15-man games in World Cups.

As a scrumhalf, he was without equal as a scavenger of the loose ball. In the book *The Chosen: The 50 Greatest Springboks of All Time*, he is aptly described as having 'feral' instincts. It goes on: 'With his long-legged loping gait and a disconcertingly flat stare out of washed-out blue-green eyes he resembled nothing so much as a rugby playing wolf, one with its competitiveness honed to an incisor-sharp point.'

Joost had an astonishing strike rate that not even Welsh rugby legend Gareth Edwards could match. At the end of 1996, after an international against Wales at Cardiff Arms Park (the Springboks won 37-20), where he established a record by scoring a hat-trick of tries, Joost asked Edwards, one of his childhood heroes, for his autograph.

Interview with Joost van der Westhuizen

Against Wales you scored a hat trick at Cardiff Arms Park – tell me about that.

That's something no one can take away from me. I'm the only international player to have scored three tries in a match at the old Cardiff Arms Park and, because the stadium no longer exists, my record can never be broken. After the game I got Gareth Edwards's autograph – he was always my hero – and he signed and wrote, 'With admiration'.

The Weekender, 21–22 March 2009

(The Springbok scrumhalf also holds the dubious test record of twice throwing passes over the head of his flyhalf that reached the third row of the stadium. One was to Jannie de Beer and the other to Louis Koen.)

Joost was big for a scrumhalf: he weighed 92 kilograms and is 1.85 metres tall – usually the build of a flanker. He was also a superb athlete, representing his province at both high jump and long jump, and was almost stupidly courageous; his head-on tackle of the giant Jonah Lomu in the 1995 Rugby World Cup final being a perfect example. He claims that instead of it having been a heroic act, he was merely, like the title of Corné Krige's book, 'in the right place at the wrong time'.

Joost's intuitive try-scoring confused rugby commentators as often as it did his teammates. 'And van der Westhuizen has the ball and ... My goodness, he's scored!' was heard by radio listeners and TV viewers on more than one occasion.

Joost was often criticised for trying to do too much on his own, for being 'selfish', a classic example of which occurred on the tour to Australia in 1993. In his first game for the Springboks against Western Australia in Perth, Joost chipped the ball on their 22-metre line, which was apparently the wrong thing to do so deep in the opposition's territory. Joost then raced through, caught the ball in the in-goal area and went down amid a heaving pile of bodies. When the dust settled, the ref stuck his arm up and signalled a try. Joost later heard that when he had kicked the ball, Ian McIntosh had jumped up and screamed, 'What is the selfish idiot doing now?' (The selfish idiot went on to score four tries in that game.)

Given his tally of tries and the number of matches in which he featured as a game-breaker, his judgement couldn't have been too flawed.

Joost was also very arrogant. 'Wherever I looked there were people telling me how amazing I was. The teams I was playing for were mostly winning and I was regularly scoring tries, so, quite frankly, I too thought I was amazing.'

He laughs. 'It's only now that my career is over and I look back that I can see what a prick I was. But my whole life was rugby and it was all going so well. And it was all I knew.'

He is probably being harsh on himself. People who were closely involved with him at the time say his arrogance was largely a filter to keep out the unwanted attentions of the masses – which, in turn, created the belief that he was arrogant because he wouldn't countenance their unsolicited attentions.

Joost is unquestionably a private person who, despite his more public persona in recent years as a socialite and TV rugby analyst, is still uncomfortable in the public eye.

Yet his arrogance cannot be completely discounted, as it has doubtless been the cause of many of his indiscretions. A blind belief in his infallibility, charm and desirability has sometimes led him to behave less than satisfactorily. This is something he acknowledges without going into detail.

And it is something he regrets. Pointing out to him that everyone has regrets and that no one was given a handbook for what they were supposed to do doesn't resonate with him.

In numerous conversations he alludes to how he was never properly coached in 'life'. He is quick to point out that he was always supported by his family – but support isn't the same as guidance. 'That's why rugby was so easy,' he says. 'There was always someone telling me what to do and what to aim for. But in life it was different. I just seemed to get a lot of signals that said I could do anything I wanted because I was Joost.'

Joost and Amor are often accused of being 'media sluts'. The facts do not support the accusation. As an example: according to Joost, he and Amor have never requested to be on the cover of any publication. 'In fact,' he says, 'no mention is ever made of how many times we have turned down such requests.' Also, he points out, they now usually appear on the front pages for all the wrong reasons.

'The unfortunate truth of it all is that we sell newspapers and magazines. Our names on their covers enormously increases their circulation.'

Another point, often conveniently forgotten, is that Amor's profession as a singer is, to a large extent, media-driven. If she wants to sell CDs, she needs to be constantly in the popular press.

Given that Joost is a legendary former rugby player, at one time an idol to millions, and Amor the pre-eminent Afrikaans female pop singer, they are often touted as *the* South African celebrity couple.

'Fine, that goes with the territory,' says Joost. 'The bit I can't handle is that so much of [what is reported] is destructive rubbish, which is manufactured by twisting the facts. Or in so many cases – I've now lost count – they simply make everything up. Then, if we want to set the record straight, *we* have to prove that they're lying.'

Without seeing burglars under the bed, he says he is convinced that a lot of his (and Amor's) troubles are born out of the Afrikaner version of tall poppy syndrome (TPS), a pejorative social attitude usually found in the UK, Australia, New Zealand and Canada.

'I liken our situation to a bunch of crayfish in a bucket,' says Joost. 'When one of them hooks his claw on the lip of the bucket to pull himself up to see how he can improve his situation, instead of copying him, all the other crayfish climb on his back and pull him down.'

His analogy is not as obscure as it first sounds; he just seems to have swapped crustaceans. The following statement appears in Wikipedia, the online encyclopaedia:

Crab mentality (sometimes also described as 'crab in a bucket syndrome') describes a way of thinking best described by the phrase 'if I can't have it, neither can you'.

Some social commentators argue that TPS is a universal phenomenon and not just a characteristic of a few countries. Perhaps it is just more common in some cultures than in others. In other words, Joost may have a point. The TPS concept originates from Aristotle's *Politics*, in which he writes, 'Periander advised Thrasybulus by cutting off the tallest ears of corn, meaning he must always put out of the way the citizens who overtop the rest.' For many of their countrymen, Joost and Amor have done too well – they have 'overtopped the rest'.

'It's all right for us to do well up to a point,' says Joost, 'but we mustn't do *too* well. If we do, then it is open season. Then we are fair game, and for some reason – or at least according to the crayfish theory – people, Afrikaners, bring us down.'

Benjamin Franklin Fairless, president of the United States Steel Corporation in the 1950s, criticised such behaviour and put the issue into perspective when he stated, 'You cannot strengthen one by weakening another; and you cannot add to the stature of a dwarf by cutting off the legs of a giant.'

Joost has another theory, which is also one of his pet hates – what he calls 'mass people'.

He explains: 'Mass people are people who, when they are in public, are loud and abrasive and pretend to know it all. You've seen and heard those guys who shout in pubs? Or maybe they are on the other side of the road and they call my name, as if we are old mates. Or sometimes, if I'm going to the toilet, they yell at me as if they know me: "Hey, Joost, just come here for a moment; we want to ask you something." Those same guys, if they encounter you in the toilet when they're on their own, don't say a word.'

He continues: 'I think that at home these guys are nobodies. So, when they're in a group in public, they show off to their friends to prove what big deals they are, knowing all along that they are nothing of the sort. They are "mass people". They only exist as people through others.'

Interview with Joost van der Westhuizen

DG: Other teams have talent, success, etc., but they don't have the same fanatical support as the Bulls. Why do you think their supporters are so fanatical?

JvdW: I think for many of those people, they only have two things in their lives. A song called 'De La Rey', and rugby. I don't think it is healthy.

The Weekender, 21 March 2009

Then, apart from the 'mass people', he talks about the 'knockers'. This is his euphemism for the Boeremafia.

Joost abruptly returns to discussing rugby. 'What no one really acknowledges,' he says, 'is that in many respects, rugby is an individual sport.'

Despite all the talk about 'team spirit', he claims people are only in the game for themselves. He cites the example of the treatment of former Springbok (1996–2001) and Free State/Cheetahs flanker André Venter. 'At one stage, he was the fittest rugby player in the world,' says Joost. 'Then he got flu and a virus infiltrated his spine and he became paralysed. He is still, to this day, in a wheelchair.'

Venter was Joost's roommate for years and he respected the big flank enormously. Joost recently visited him, and Venter said it really got him down when he first became ill when none of his Free State teammates visited him or kept in touch. He mentioned that players from other provinces visit him, but that not one of his former teammates from his own province makes any effort.

Joost shakes his head and says, 'He is the most amazing person. Early on in his illness, I went to visit him and they had recently fitted him with callipers. He was so excited to be walking again. He said to me, "You know, Joost, the passage outside is 50 metres long. The first time I tried to walk it, you know what? It took me

55 minutes. I'm now doing it in 11 minutes." I just kept quiet. I mean, this guy was so happy with that little achievement. Yet none of his old mates from his Free State playing days have anything to do with him.'

Says Joost: 'I still see some of my guys, but not often. I see Kobus Wiese [former Springbok lock] and Breyton Paulse [former Springbok wing] when he visits from Cape Town. Of course I see everyone when we have reunions and when we play the Springbok Legends games, but rugby definitely isn't a big team game when it comes to how things turn out in later life.

'Let me explain about Springbok Legends rugby, because that was one of the good things to come out of the game in my time. The concept is John Allan's [former Springbok 1993–1996 and Sharks hooker] baby. He is now the CEO of Springbok Legends. He wanted to start something through which former players could give something back to rugby. So they built sport academies in the townships with all the facilities to teach various sports to the kids. The plan is to build about 400 of these academies. We want to take the kids off the streets and give them all-round rugby, soccer and netball coaching, and to provide them with food and direction [in life].

'What happens is that local teams – say, for example, Orkney – will invite the Legends to a match. Then we will go, maybe have a golf day so that they can raise money, and we'll hold a rugby clinic for the youngsters in the area. We will then play a match against the local team.'

He laughs and says, 'The games are quite funny. When they start, there is always some youngster who wants to make his name and have a crack at a Springbok. Well, it usually takes about five or six minutes to put him in his place. I mean, it's silly; a lot of them hadn't been born when we were playing for the Boks and now they want to have a go at us? So, using our experience, or just by giving them a good old-fashioned *klap*, we let them know politely that if what they want to do isn't legal, they had better stop.'

The Blue Bulls supporter

To a committed Blue Bulls rugby supporter like Sakkie de Kok, rugby is not a religion, as has so often been reported. It is profoundly more serious.

But despite eating, sleeping and breathing rugby, naming his daughters after the Bulls' front row and possessing all the team branding, Sakkie is surprisingly unbiased. This is reflected in the admirable way he loudly and generously applauds the opposition whenever the Bulls have beaten them. And if by some fluke the visitors actually win – inevitably the fault of the referee – he doesn't complain. He simply makes plans to emigrate.

Strangely, Sakkie doesn't tend to *watch* the matches he so devotedly attends. He prefers instead to purchase beer and food and discuss team selection with strangers while wading in the toilets. (In the 'old days', when alcohol was banned at stadiums, Sakkie resourcefully injected oranges with vodka or brandy, or both. Later, when no fruit was available and he was about to inject himself, Loftus Versfeld conveniently began selling booze.)

If Sakkie does make it to the stands, he participates in vigorous in-your-face blue-flag waving. (Secretly he prefers the old South African flag, but it has been blacklisted.) He often accompanies these exertions with cheerful and harmless chants of abuse to make people think he knows the words to the national anthem. And if the game becomes boring, he resorts to giving the person in front of him a determined, encouraging blow on the back.

In solidarity with the magnificently honed physiques of his heroes on the field, Sakkie de Kok takes great pride in his appearance and maintains the obligatory belly of a true supporter in showroom condition. He keeps his light-blue shirt, light-blue shorts and light-blue socks immaculate. Before every match, he assiduously polishes his light-blue plastic helmet – the one with the horns.

Sakkie is well aware that knowledge of the rules of rugby can be a distinct handicap when criticising the referee – especially if the ref has made the correct decision – so he has made a point of not knowing them. And sometimes, just for the fun of it, Sakkie likes to occupy a seat other than the one for which he has a ticket. He adds to this little mischief by good-naturedly shouting, 'SIT! SIT DOWN!' when the ticket-holder for the seat arrives.

In the interests of sportsmanship, Sakkie recommends opposition supporters don't go to games. But if attendance is absolutely unavoidable, he believes fairness dictates that no colours should be worn that could identify spectators as opposition supporters, as this gives the visiting team an unfair advantage. And although cheering for foreign sides is perfectly acceptable to him, Sakkie is of the opinion that it should be done mutely, with the minimum of accompanying physical movement, so as not to distract his team.

Intriguingly, when black players in his team excel, Sakkie immediately experiences severe colour-blindness. However, the condition is only temporary and normal sight is swiftly restored when a 'previously disadvantaged' player doesn't do something astonishingly spectacular each time he gets the ball.

Sakkie de Kok, dyed-in-the-wool Bulls rugby supporter, is devoted, passionate and united with others of his ilk in his unwavering conviction that soccer players are poofters and rugby is more important than life itself.

From a series called 'SA Stereotypes' by David Gemmell – as published in Anytime *magazine, 2009.*

7

Writing Joost's book IV

Joost points out that during his Springbok career, he served under no fewer than seven coaches.

'That's great,' I say. 'We can divide your career into coaches, as opposed to the more conventional years.'

He agrees. We are sitting on the balcony of his house in Dainfern Valley. His son Jordan runs past with a basketball under his arm. When I arrived, the kid was terribly upset because I parked almost directly under his hoop, which I hadn't seen because it's fixed quite high up on the wall next to the garage door.

With a smile on his face, he waved his little arms and frantically gesticulated at me to park my car elsewhere. It was somehow reminiscent of his father behind a Springbok ruck. Completely misreading the situation – I thought he was thrilled to see his dad's NBF and happily waved back – I only realised when he stopped smiling that he was furious with me for ruining his game.

Joost has just returned from three nights away in the bush, where he was on a combined hunting/business trip.

'So, how was it?' I inquire.

'Did you hear about that farmer who last week ran over his kids by accident and they died?' Joost asks.

'I saw something about it on the posters, but, no, I didn't read about it. Why?'

'It was his farm we were hunting on.'

'Oh God ... Was he there?'

'Yes, he was with us the whole time. It was tricky. Most of the time, no one knew what to do or what to talk to him about. Then one evening he sat with us around the fire and said he needed people

around him. He said he couldn't be on his own. But later, while he was talking to me, he would suddenly look away every now and then and just stare into the distance.'

I don't think it appropriate to comment on the relative merits of Joost's own world-class stare. 'It was very difficult,' Joost continues. 'What can you say to someone who has just been through such a tragedy?'

'What actually happened?' I ask.

'Apparently he was driving this old farm vehicle and his kids were on the front seat next to him and the door flew open and they fell out – and he rode over them. I was a passenger in the same vehicle, an old truck, and you can't believe it, but the door kept opening as we were driving along. I had to pull it closed. The bizarre thing was that it was hard to get the door open to get into the truck. The whole thing was horrible. When I got home last night the kids were in the kitchen with Amor and when they saw me they ran and jumped into my arms, and I just cried and cried.'

It takes a few moments before it seems appropriate to talk about something as comparatively inconsequential as rugby.

When we do try to do some work, a new problem presents itself. 'I don't know if I'm depressed or something because of the trip,' Joost says, 'but you won't believe me – I can't remember a bloody thing about any of the coaches. It's like they all blend into one. I don't understand it.'

Not entirely sure if he is pulling my leg or if he is just trying to avoid working, I suggest we pop down the road to see my psychologist friend Nick Christodolou. Perhaps he can help. (I occasionally feel that Joost needs his memory jogged about you-know-what, but instead resign myself to having my socks blown off in the last chapter – which is still a long way off.)

Unusually, Nick is in and can see us right away.

At first the conversation between the three of us focuses on the tragedy that had befallen Joost's hunting host. I, too, have started to get depressed and am just beginning to wonder if my memory, which is already like a sieve, will also disappear, when Nick gets up and walks over to Joost.

'Look at the end of my pen,' he says in a monotone, as he moves the pen rhythmically from side to side, just a foot or so from Joost's face. He tells Joost that he is feeling drowsy and will soon fall asleep.

This is a completely unexpected development, but it doesn't throw my amnesic NBF. Smiling smugly, he says, 'Sorry, Nick, but people have tried to hypnotise me before and they couldn't do it … zzz.' Joost is still smiling smugly as he falls fast asleep. It is absolutely fascinating.

The minute Joost is asleep, Nick tells him that his brain is going to go and fetch the thoughts he needs from where they are stored in his psyche.

I must confess, Nick sounds like one of those stage hypnotists I have always believed to be con artists. But there is nothing fake about the sleeping Joost. It also seems so remarkably commonplace, as though putting someone to sleep is an everyday affair. Does that make sense? Perhaps you have to see it yourself.

'The minute you have fetched those memories, you will lift the little finger of your right hand,' Nick instructs the comatose Joost. Except, he calls it a pinkie; 'Your right pinkie,' are his exact words.

Fascinated, I focus on that pinkie. Will it move? For 20 minutes Nick repeats his little refrain until, suddenly, Joost's pinkie develops a life of its own.

Slowly it raises itself until it looks like a small, erect penis. As I study it, I presume the phallic connotation it prompts no doubt stems from the universal sign females employ to indicate that someone has a small willy – not that I've ever actually seen a girl make it …

However, I digress. At this point Nick brings Joost around. At first no one says a word, and then Joost, looking somewhat drowsy, says, 'Sorry … I think I nodded off.'

'You were hypnotised,' I say. 'Do you have any idea how long you were under?'

'A few moments,' he replies, then suddenly looks disconcerted. 'Did I say anything?'

I want to tease him and tell him he had confessed to all sorts of crimes, but think better of it. It doesn't seem fair. 'No, you didn't say anything. It was amazing; you were absolutely gone for about 25 minutes.'

Nick smiles and says, 'You won't actually feel any different for a while, but later, when you need to, you will remember everything about your rugby that you would have remembered in the normal course of events. In one session I can't make you remember stuff you have long forgotten, but the more recent memories will come back to you.'

I make a mental note to see if I can perhaps get Joost to see Nick in future on another little issue ...

8

Ian McIntosh

During his 10-year international rugby career, Joost played under seven coaches (and 11 flyhalves). In any other industry, so many changes in management over such a relatively short period of time would be seen, at best, as bungling and, at worst, as catastrophic. In many respects, it was. (When Joost wasn't playing for the Springboks, he also had coaches for Super League and Currie Cup rugby, which, mind-bogglingly, added at least another eight to the mix.)

On 12 March 1993, Ian McIntosh was appointed Springbok coach, supposedly until the 1995 Rugby World Cup. Joost didn't know the former Zimbabwean, but because he had been the Natal coach, Joost assumed he would be sticking with his regular Natal scrumhalf, Robert du Preez, for the Boks. Joost was right.

It was extremely frustrating, though it comforted Joost somewhat that he had a solid excuse when he wasn't chosen for the test team. 'I used to say to myself, "*Ag*, I won't be in the test side because of Ian Mac and Robert du Preez," and that made it tolerable.'

In many respects, Joost blames his attitude on his Afrikaner upbringing; it was easier to use cronyism as an excuse than to accept that perhaps he wasn't good enough or admit that he still had lots to learn. Du Preez was far more experienced than the arrogant young Joost and much better suited to the Boks' game plan at the time. However, Joost simply wasn't able to bring himself to say, 'I'm prepared to learn.'

In 1993, Joost toured Australia with the Springboks under

Year	Vs	Score	Scrumhalf	Flyhalf	Captain	Tries
1993		**SA-Other**				
	France	20-20	Robert du Preez	Hennie le Roux	François Pienaar	
	France	17-18	Robert du Preez	Hennie le Roux	François Pienaar	
	Australia	19-12	Robert du Preez	Joel Stransky	François Pienaar	
	Australia	20-28	Robert du Preez	Joel Stransky	François Pienaar	
	Australia	12-19	Robert du Preez	Joel Stransky	François Pienaar	
	Argentina	29-26	Joost	Joel Stransky	François Pienaar	1
	Argentina	52-23	Joost	Henry Honiball	François Pienaar	1
1994						
	England	15-32	Joost	Hennie le Roux	François Pienaar	
	England	27-9	Johan Roux	Hennie le Roux	François Pienaar	
	New Zealand	14-22	Johan Roux	Hennie le Roux	François Pienaar	
	New Zealand	9-13	Johan Roux	Hennie le Roux	François Pienaar	
	New Zealand	18-18	Johan Roux	Hennie le Roux	François Pienaar	
Tests: won 4, lost 6, drew 2						

McIntosh. He made his Springbok debut against Western Australia, but didn't play in any of the three tests. It was only later, when he went to Argentina with the Boks, when he finally played in an international.

'You only become a Springbok,' says Joost, 'when you actually run on the field and play. Sitting on the bench and being in the squad doesn't count. I sat on the bench twice before we went to Australia, but, until I played, I wasn't a Springbok and couldn't wear my Springbok blazer.'

McIntosh required his Springboks to sign a code of honour.

Springbok Code of Honour

I, *Joost van der Westhuizen*, solemnly pledge that I shall, at all times, wear the Springbok colours and conduct myself with pride and dignity;

Ensure that all my actions are worthy of the proud traditions of Springbok rugby;

Place the Springbok team and its interests above my own ambitions;

Never surrender whilst enjoying the privilege of wearing the green and gold;

At all times remain humble in Victory and dignified in Defeat.

Before Joost became a Springbok, he was a Sevens Springbok. The Springbok Sevens squad was announced after the National Sevens Tournament in Stellenbosch in 1992, and Joost was chosen. 'That was awesome,' he says. 'And it came as a surprise. I was still young, just a boy, and I didn't expect it. Then, in 1993, I was chosen to sit on the bench for the Springboks (the 15-man team) for the incoming tour against France. For me it was just reaching one goal after the other, so I didn't mind sitting on the bench. That was one of my goals – to sit on the bench for the Springboks.'

Although he says he didn't mind not going on the field for the two games against France, he felt he was a step closer to playing. 'I suppose I had mixed feelings. I was pleased when the guys did well but I was sorry I didn't play.' Given that South Africa drew one game and lost the other against the French, perhaps it wasn't the best time to make his debut ...

And then he was chosen for the tour Down Under. According to Joost, he started off a very quiet traveller on the Australian tour and was catatonic by the time it ended – all born out of being unable to speak English, being one of the new boys and completely lacking social confidence. This he blames on his conservative background.

Not surprisingly, during that 1993 tour, the Australian commentators had a lot of difficulty pronouncing his name. None of them could get it right. They called him Oost or Juice and came up with some fantastic renditions of his surname.

During one mid-week game, played up in the north-east of Brisbane in sugar country, at a place called Mackay, Joost was on the bench. Late in the game he went on as a substitute. Hugh Bladen, the South African commentator who travelled with the Springboks on that tour, tells how his fellow commentator, an Australian, said, 'Oh my God, I was hoping this wasn't going to happen.'

Looking at his team list, the local man grimaced and, still slightly inebriated from a too-liquid lunch, said, 'Ah, the South Africans are putting on that impressive young scrumhalf ... Juiced van da Westahousehazen.'

The next tour he went on, Joost made every effort to be more amenable to his fellow travellers and the people he met, but admits frankly that he hadn't exactly been the life and soul of the party in Australia.

Joost recalls that McIntosh changed the Boks' method of initiation.

'The tradition,' he says, 'was for the debutants to wait outside the initiation room and then go in one at a time. In the room, they would have to stand on a chair, down a beer and tell a joke – at which no one would laugh. Then every member of the touring party, using an open hand, would hit the new man on the left cheek of his bum. So, first round, I got 30 shots. Next I had to tell them my life history, and I got another 30 shots. Of course they found something wrong with what I said, and in the end I took a total of 90 hits on my left cheek.'

Apparently McIntosh thought it was too 'hectic' and worried that his players could be injured. So he changed the 'punishment' to three strokes of a cane. The cane was symbolic of the one Dr Danie Craven used to walk with. 'Before they whacked the guys,' says Joost, 'they would tell them about Doc Craven's dog, which was called Bliksem. And then they would bliksem the guy using a cane ...'

Management was also initiated. 'If you wanted to wear the Springbok blazer, you had to get initiated,' says Joost. 'But management's initiation was always less vicious.'

In his debut match for Pretoria University's first team, Joost scored a try. In his debut match for Northern Transvaal, he scored a try. So it seemed only fitting – and inevitable – when, in the 11th minute of his debut test for the Springboks against Argentina (Springboks 29, Argentina 26), yes, he scored a try. (Amazingly, in his first game for the Springboks against Western Australia, also Joel Stransky's first game as a Bok, Joost scored four tries. An auspicious start to what later became one of the longest Springbok test careers and a portent of his future as the highest try-scoring Springbok in history.)

The relationship between Ian McIntosh and Van der Westhuizen was one of mutual suspicion. At that stage in Joost's life he was quiet to the point of surliness. Combined with a brash overconfidence that stemmed from a total belief in his own ability, it didn't make for easy communication between the young Afrikaner and the English coach.

However, Joost remembers McIntosh saying, as clearly as if it were yesterday, 'Just stay calm. You'll get your day.' To which the arrogant scrumhalf sullenly replied, 'Ja, whatever ...'

'When I look back,' says Joost today, 'Ian Mac was a brilliant coach. At the time I thought I knew too much to appreciate what he was doing. Mind you, you have to remember he was my first English coach. Up until then I had only had Afrikaans coaches.'

Joost recounts a 'Mac' story from the tour of Australia. One morning on the tour bus, McIntosh told the squad that he was pissed off because he had been called to reception after breakfast, where he'd found an extremely attractive young lady waiting for him. As he walked up to the desk, she stared at him, then turned to the receptionist and said, 'This isn't Ian McIntosh.'

'Yes, I am,' said Ian.

The girl studied him carefully and said, 'Either I was paralytic-ally drunk last night, or you are *not* Ian McIntosh.'

'Which one of you bastards,' asked Ian of the laughing busload of Boks, 'told her you were me?'

Joost's time under McIntosh was blighted by a bizarre family tragedy. One weekend Izak Terblanche, the 18-year-old brother of Joost's fiancée Marlene Terblanche, borrowed Joost's Toyota double cab to go to the coast with some friends for a post-matric holiday. When they got to their destination late in the evening, Izak phoned to say that they'd arrived safely. However, at about four in the morning, Joost received another call, this time from the police, informing him that there had been a fatal accident.

Izak had been driving. Apparently they had gone out to buy supplies when, on a treacherous corner, the vehicle flipped and the roof was ripped off. Izak was killed instantly, as were two other boys. However, there was some confusion as to which of the boys had died with Izak, because the bodies were unrecognis-able. Fortunately some ID books that had spilt from the luggage were lying among the wreckage.

It was only after Joost had informed two sets of parents that their sons had been killed that it was discovered that the ID books had belonged to two boys who had actually changed places with the two in the double cab. Joost had informed the wrong parents that their sons were dead. Despite the obvious joy the parents of the surviving boys felt at this startling revelation, they were also furious with the messenger for putting them through such anguish.

'I have never felt such an idiot,' says Joost.

In June 1994, after the test against England in Pretoria, which the Boks lost 15-32 (and which was Joost's first international against one of the 'big' rugby nations, as he puts it), McIntosh was walking towards the tunnel when an Afrikaans spectator yelled at him, 'Ian Mac, coach, please save us!'

'As Mac turned to smile at him,' says Joost, 'the guy screamed, "RETIRE!"'

McIntosh did not have to take the unwelcome advice – he was fired after a losing tour to New Zealand.

9

Kitch Christie

Joost played 11 of Kitch Christie's unbeaten run of 14 tests. Two of the matches he missed were against the minnows Canada and Romania in the 1995 World Cup group stage; the other was Christie's first game in charge of the Boks, against Argentina.

'He was a fantastic coach,' Joost says. 'He was straightforward and honest – he always let you know where you stood. He moulded us into a team that was just like a family. Everyone was there for each other. There were no individuals – it was all team, team, team. "Look in the mirror," he would say. "You can never fool yourselves."'

Christie endeared himself to Joost early on when, upon taking over from Ian McIntosh as coach of the Springboks, he sent the squad on a training run at The Wanderers Golf Course. 'Right,' he said, 'let's see what you can do.'

As it was the first run under a new coach, there was an unstated but fierce determination on the part of all the players to impress. So they ran as fast as they could.

On their return, unmoved by their efforts, Christie said, 'Right, guys. Now we have a benchmark of what you can do. In future you will never do this run slower than you did it today.' The subtle cheek of the ploy appealed to Joost.

It also showed him how Christie's mind worked, which later stood him in good stead on the eve of a test against Australia.

Joost had been called in to see the coach, who asked him, 'Are you better than George Gregan [the Australian scrumhalf]?'

'I am,' said Joost.

'Good. So how are you going to handle him?'

48

Kitch Christie

Year	Vs	Score	Scrumhalf	Flyhalf	Captain	Tries
1994		SA-Other				
	Argentina	42-22	Johan Roux	Joel Stransky	François Pienaar	
	Argentina	46-26	Joost	Joel Stransky	François Pienaar	1
	Scotland	34-10	Joost	Hennie le Roux	François Pienaar	2
	Wales	20-12	Joost	Hennie le Roux	François Pienaar	
1995						
	Samoa	60-8	Joost	Joel Stransky	François Pienaar	
	Australia	27-18	Joost	Joel Stransky	François Pienaar	
	Romania	21-18	Johan Roux	Hennie le Roux	Adriaan Richter	
	Canada	20-0	Johan Roux	Joel Stransky	François Pienaar	
	Samoa	42-14	Joost	Hennie le Roux	François Pienaar	
	France	19-15	Joost	Joel Stransky	François Pienaar	
	New Zealand	15-12	Joost	Joel Stransky	François Pienaar	
	Wales	40-11	Joost	Joel Stransky	François Pienaar	
	Italy	40-21	Joost	Joel Stransky	François Pienaar	
	England	24-14	Joost	Joel Stransky	François Pienaar	1
Tests: won 14, lost 0						

In a previous life, Joost's answer would have been something along the lines of 'I'll dominate him from the start; pressure him; let him know I'm there, etc., etc.' Instead, he replied, 'I'll just stick to the game plan and do what we agreed in practice.'

Right answer.

At other times Joost found Christie's idiosyncratic behaviour a bit harder to handle – like the time the coach roasted a couple of players, including Joost, in front of the whole team for drinking and staying out late the night before. Joost objected to being lectured, as he had changed his mind and, instead of partying, had gone to bed.

He put his hand up to mention this to the irate Christie, who, before Joost could utter a word, responded by telling the nonplussed scrumhalf to 'Shut up! Just shut up! Don't talk back to me!'

Memorably, the night before the 1995 World Cup final, Kitch walked into the team room and gave a surprisingly short team talk – just one or two comments – and then handed each player a copy of a poem.

The Man in the Glass[*]

When you get what you want in your struggles for self
And the world makes you king for a day,
Just go to a mirror and look at yourself
And see what that man has to say.

For it isn't your father or mother or wife
Whose judgment upon you must pass,
The fellow whose verdict counts most in your life
Is the one staring back from the glass.

Some people might think you're a straight-shooting chum
And call you a wonderful guy.

---

[*] The poem handed out by Kitch Christie was not the original version. The original poem, called 'The Guy in the Glass', was written by Dale Wimbrow in 1934, and is reproduced on page 235.

But the man in the glass says you're only a bum
If you can't look him straight in the eye.

He's the fellow to please, never mind all the rest
For he's with you clear to the end
And you've passed your most dangerous test
If the guy in the glass is your friend.

You may fool the whole world down the pathway of years
And get pats on the back as you pass
But your final reward will be heartache and tears
If you've cheated the man in the glass.

Kitch Christie had some interesting quirks. In *Kitch – Triumph of a Decent Man*, Rudolf Straeuli tells how, in his pursuit of covering every detail before a match, Christie would phone Disneyland in the US for weather forecasts; according to the coach, they 'were the most scientific in the world'. In three years they only got it wrong once – for the 1995 World Cup semi-final against France (a day that almost put paid to the Springboks' World Cup hopes due to the heavy rainfall). Straeuli says: 'It became a standing joke among the players to ask the coach whom he had spoken to that day – was it Mickey Mouse or Donald Duck?'

Another aspect of Christie's coaching the players grew to enjoy was his obsession with fitness. 'In the end, he couldn't make us any fitter, because he couldn't make us tired,' says Joost. 'If I remember correctly, at that time my resting pulse was 38 beats per minute. Whatever he asked us to do, we did extra. If he said do 40 press-ups, we would do 60.'

A little-known fact about the extraordinary Christie is that when the putative World Rugby Corporation tried to take over the professional game in 1996, he was influential in the Springboks deciding to align themselves with SARFU (South African Rugby Football Union). In the book *The Rugby War*, author

Peter FitzSimons tells how, at a meeting of the Springbok players, Kitch Christie finally said his piece.

> 'I've kept out of it to this point,' one of the players remembers their mentor saying, 'because I've always thought it was your business what you do. But now I'm asking you to do what you must know is the right thing. I want you to sign with SARFU, for the team, for the country, for yourselves, for what you have already achieved.'

Sadly, throughout his coaching career with the Springboks, Kitch Christie was fighting cancer; among other things, this meant he had to undergo chemotherapy. 'We could always tell when he'd had his latest bout of chemo,' smiles Joost, 'because of the way he would rough us up at practice.' Although he never discussed it, Christie had chronic lymphoma that became chronic lymphatic leukaemia.

In his autobiography, François Pienaar recalls Christie's last game in charge of the Springboks, a 24-14 victory over England at Twickenham on 18 November 1995. Christie, whose health had visibly deteriorated, joined the team huddle and stood between Pienaar and James Dalton. 'The usual end to such a Springbok huddle is for the players to squeeze each other and shout "Bokke!"' says Pienaar. 'James and I squeezed the coach and later discovered that we'd fractured two of his ribs. He never said a word.'

Says Springbok lock Kobus Wiese: '[Kitch] was our most successful coach. I don't think there has ever been another un-defeated coach. And his people skills were fantastic. He taught us that it was important for us to do well not only because that was [the reason] we were training, but in order to become better human beings, better citizens [as well]. This was more important than the sport; there was something much bigger than the game.

'Let me give you an example. Take a guy like James Small. In South Africa, if somebody is rebellious, we call them "very different" when, actually, they are "kak-makers",' Wiese laughs. 'So Kitch called in the "very different" James Small and said, "James, you are a good player and we want you in the team. But it will be on the team's terms, not yours. You decide." James said, "No problem." And he played his best rugby under Kitch. Actually, if I was a coach, I would pick 15 "very different" players, because they are the guys who fight to win and never give up.'

James Small concurs: 'Kitch was something else. I'd been fishing with him, but when he first became coach he kicked me out of the side for drinking on a Friday night. So the first call I got from the new Springbok coach was to boot me out of the side. But he was also incredible; an amazing man.'

According to Springbok centre Hennie le Roux, who was a member of the 1995 World Cup–winning team, 'Kitch was a pretty structured type of guy without being complicated. I really enjoyed him as well. And, of course, his record was amazing.'

World Cup Champion flyhalf and kicker of the world's 'most important' drop goal, Joel Stransky, says, '[Kitch] was a unique man; a quiet, reserved man. You had to do something very special to earn his respect. I remember the first time I met him on the training ground at the Wanderers. He came to talk to me about which foot I took off on. He watched me and then told me to put my other foot forward. I didn't understand what he was getting at, so I said, "But Kitch ..." and he immediately said, "Don't ever call me Kitch. You either call me Coach or Mr Christie, but don't ever call me Kitch." There was that definite line of respect. Eventually it did become "Coachy",' Stransky smiles, 'but there was that line. He was an amazing man.'

In 1997, Kitch returned from retirement to coach Northern Transvaal. When, just before his appointment, doubt was cast on his health, he said, 'You are hiring me for my mind, not my body.'

Only weeks later, while in hospital, Kitch suffered perhaps the lowest blow of his career, when Northerns' president Hentie

Serfontein visited him to tell him his services were no longer required.

'He fired me like a dog,' said Christie in typically outspoken fashion.

At his funeral in 1998, the whole of the 1995 World Cup squad walked behind the coffin. Afterwards, each went his own way to shed a few tears. 'One of the saddest funerals I have ever attended,' says Joost.

'I'm not afraid of dying; it's just that I prefer living.'
– GEORGE MOIR 'KITCH' CHRISTIE, 1940–1998

The Rugby World Cup

In 1987, the International Rugby Board organised an inaugural Rugby World Cup (RWC) to be contested by the rugby-playing nations of the world. Ironically, because of the sports boycott against South Africa at the time, the tournament would not include one of the pre-eminent teams in world rugby, the Springboks. It was a sore point, and one that Louis Luyt couldn't resist mentioning in his speech at the official dinner following South Africa's narrow victory over New Zealand in the 1995 RWC. Not renowned for his subtlety, Luyt declared that, in his opinion, had they been allowed to play, South Africa would have won the previous two World Cups as well. The All Blacks responded equally subtly by walking out of the room.

The first RWC was hosted by Australia and New Zealand, and is now contested every four years. Winners of the tournament are awarded the Webb Ellis Cup, or Trophy, named after William Webb Ellis (24 November 1806–24 January 1872), generally credited as the founder of the game of rugby.

The story of how Webb Ellis invented the game might almost certainly be false, but his name will forever be firmly entrenched in the folklore of the game of Rugby Union.

Even if Webb Ellis did introduce running with the ball in hand (for which there is no evidence), the reason football (soccer) split into two codes was over the issue of 'hacking' – tackling a player by kicking him in the shins.

The practice was banned in soccer, but for a while allowed in rugby – although today it is banned in both games. Not that banning 'hacking' necessarily completely eliminated kicking, or, for that matter, punching, eye-gouging, biting, spitting, trampling and other attractive conduct from either sport.

The fact that hacking was allowed in rugby, at least initially, but banned in football gave birth to the concept of rugby being a game for hooligans played by gentlemen (players tended to be better educated), while soccer was a game for gentlemen played by hooligans.

Back to the RWC – the Webb Ellis Cup is silver, gilded in gold, stands 38 centimetres tall and is supported by two cast scroll handles. According to Wikipedia, the trophy was crafted by Garrard's Crown Jewellers in 1906 and modelled on a 1906 cup made by Carrington and Co. of London, which was a Victorian design of a 1740 cup by Paul de Lamerie. So it is a marvellous piece of antiquity.

And despite the trophy being of somewhat diminutive dimensions, being able to legitimately lift the hallowed cup in victory is hugely difficult. The relatively few rugby players who have managed the enviable feat will happily attest to the obstacles that need to be overcome and the sacrifices required.

The inaugural RWC tournament was won by New Zealand, captained by scrumhalf David Kirk (now MBE), against France at Eden Park in Auckland (29-9). Since then, the Webb Ellis Cup has been won twice by Australia (1991, 1999), twice by South Africa (1995, 2007) and once by England (2003).

Joost van der Westhuizen played in three World Cups. In 1995 he was part of the winning Springbok team, and in 1999 he captained South Africa to the semi-finals in England. In 2003 he played in the RWC in Australia, after which he retired from rugby when the Springboks lost in the quarter-finals of the competition.

10

Rugby World Cup 1995

Originally, Kitch Christie wanted to choose Johan Roux as his first-choice scrumhalf for the 1995 World Cup. In *Kitch – Triumph of a Decent Man*, he says that his impression of Joost van der Westhuizen was that the rangy Blue Bull was 'an extremely talented player, but he was unpredictable. He might win you a game with a moment of brilliance but then lose you the next one. I was very concerned that this kind of player, in a key position, could prove a liability in a knockout tournament like the World Cup. What would happen if he suffered a bad day, in, say, the quarter-final?'

However, after a tour to Britain during which Joost produced brilliant performances in tests against Scotland (SA 34, Scotland 10) and Wales (SA 20, Wales 12) and had many solid outings in the other matches, Christie decided that Joost would be his scrumhalf.

Joost trained as hard as he had ever trained. 'The Boks missed out on the 1987 and 1991 World Cups,' says Joost, 'so we knew this would be a fantastic opportunity to show the world what it had been missing. Also, we would be competing in front of home crowds, which, while wonderful, also put enormous pressure on us.'

Because they had failed to qualify for the Super 10 tournament in 1995, Northern Transvaal decided to tour Britain. They won five of the six matches they played, with Joost scoring four tries.

His game had come on in leaps and bounds – literally. However, it wasn't all plain sailing for the increasingly cocky scrumhalf. After a game against Western Samoa at Ellis Park, in which the

Springboks thrashed the islanders 60-8, on 15 April 1995, the *Pretoria News* carried a report by Lester Mills that contained a comment from the Springbok coach: '"In conditions where he should have revelled, scrumhalf Joost van der Westhuizen was at his best disappointing and his form disturbing," Christie said.'

Mills continued: 'So while most pundits would automatically be pencilling the Blue Bull halfback into their Springbok World Cup first-choice line-up, the 24-year-old prolific try-scorer may find himself having to earn the right all over again …'

Joost reckons it was one of Christie's ploys to bring him down to earth. 'I was getting a bit *windgat*,' he laughs. 'I was just so bloody keen to do well and for us to win the World Cup at home. I think Kitch wrote the article and asked Lester to run it.'

On 30 April 1995, Morné du Plessis, the recently appointed team manager for the 1995 Springbok World Cup campaign, announced the Springbok squad – Joost van der Westhuizen was included as scrumhalf. 'I felt unbelievable – suddenly I was reaching my topmost goals,' he recalls, 'the ones I was almost too scared to dream about. I was also more motivated than before – if that was possible,' he laughs. 'I suddenly had the urge to rush out and do an extra bit of training …'

Interestingly, he adds, 'There was also a vague sense of disbelief. In a strange way I still felt this couldn't actually be happening to me, despite all the hard work [I'd put in] and everything that had gone before. But then it was all replaced by a determined, nervous sense of confidence. I don't know how else to describe it.'

For the Springboks, there were two roads to the final: the low road, which meant that they would meet teams like New Zealand and England in the quarter- or semi-finals; or the high road, which meant that they would play against teams like Samoa, France and Argentina. The decision would effectively be made by the result of their first game against Australia, which would take place at Newlands in Cape Town. They had to win to get on the high road. It was a daunting task that lay ahead.

But not everything was serious and intense in the run-up to the game. Kobus Wiese remembers how he, Rudolf Straeuli, James Dalton and Balie Swart went down to the Victoria & Alfred Waterfront for dinner one night. 'As we left the restaurant,' the massive lock says, 'a fishing boat pulled in and a fisherman gave Rudolf a fresh snoek "for luck". We didn't know what Straeuli was going to do with it, but it was late, so we returned to the hotel. Rudolf then put the snoek into Pieter Hendriks's bed with its head on the pillow.'

Apparently when Hendriks got into his room, he didn't want to put the lights on and disturb his roommates, so he climbed into bed in the dark. 'Well, Pieter gets nauseous easily and was immediately sick all over the place,' Kobus laughs. 'That snoek then travelled from room to room for a week. In the end it was decomposing. It was terrible!'

Nobody who was at Newlands that Thursday 25 May 1995 will ever forget the excitement and roar that greeted President Nelson Mandela as he walked out to open the 1995 Rugby World Cup. When the crowd, by then almost crazed with excitement, started chanting 'Nelson! Nelson! Nelson! Nelson ...', there wasn't a dry eye in the stadium.

It is with great pride and pleasure that I welcome you to the opening of the Rugby World Cup in South Africa. There can be no greater expression of a nation's pride, nor nobler path to universal understanding than for the cream of its youth to compete on the playing field. It is through their love of the game, their desire to succeed through skill and sacrifice, that mighty links are forged.

In this spirit of healthy rivalry, let play begin. And may the better team win. — NELSON MANDELA, PRESIDENT OF THE REPUBLIC OF SOUTH AFRICA

White English liberals and conservative Afrikaners stood alongside their black, Indian, Asian and coloured fellow South Africans and combined as one to chant the name of the former terrorist, political prisoner, struggle hero, ANC cadre, comrade – the tall, grey-haired, first black president of South Africa, Nelson Mandela. It was a spontaneous outbreak of unity, the likes of which the planet will probably never see again.

After that, the kick-off was almost an anticlimax. Australian flyhalf Michael Lynagh further exacerbated the anticlimactic mood for South African supporters when he went over for a try. At half-time, the score was South Africa 6, Australia 14.

But then, three minutes after the break, when Springbok wing Pieter Hendriks ran around David Campese – probably the finest player ever to represent Australia – and scored in the corner, the Newlands crowd's spirits were revived and the place went berserk.

The packed stadium's rekindled and unbridled enthusiasm was mostly focused on Springbok flyhalf Joel Stransky. In what for him must have been a dream start to the World Cup, he scored in every way possible on a rugby field. Later, Joel was asked:

In the first game of the 95 World Cup against Australia, you scored a drop goal, a penalty and a try; did you see that as a good omen for the tournament?
No, I'm not at all superstitious. The only thing I was superstitious about when I played was the way I packed my bag. I use to pack it in a certain way from the bottom up; but that was the only thing … Oh, there was one other thing. When we went onto the field I wouldn't step on the lines (laughs); of course that didn't apply during the game. But that definitely was it. So no, I didn't really see my scoring in that game as an omen.

When the final whistle blew, the score read South Africa 27, Australia 17. The high road beckoned.

In the remaining pool games against Canada and Romania, coach Kitch Christie made a point of using his whole squad. It was a calculated risk. He knew that in doing so he would reinforce the loyalty of all the players and he could rest a key player like Van der Westhuizen. But he also knew that if they lost, he would be forever vilified for fielding a weakened side. However, Kitch Christie operated on fundamentally simple beliefs. He knew instinctively that if he placed his faith in his players, they would not let him down.

South Africa defeated Romania 21-8, also at Newlands, with only four of the 15 players who had beaten Australia in the opening game. The next match, against Canada in Port Elizabeth, was blighted by a brawl on the touchline, which resulted in three players being sent off. Just before the fight broke out, Joost had gone on the right wing as a replacement for the injured Gavin Johnson. Fortunately he stayed put as the players slugged it out on the other side of the field.

The game ended with South Africa winning 20-0 and James Dalton and Pieter Hendriks effectively out of the World Cup. Thirty-day suspensions had become standard for any red-carded player.

South Africa's quarter-final opponents were Western Samoa. The match was played at Ellis Park, where the Springboks had beaten the islanders 60-8 six weeks earlier. Again the Springboks won – the score was 42-12 at the final whistle. But this game was also blighted by an unpleasant incident, and this time it involved Joost van der Westhuizen.

Both packs were furiously scrabbling for possession when the Samoan eighth man and captain, Pat Lam, stood up and began gesturing viciously at the Springbok scrumhalf. Joost responded in perfect imitation of the wildly gesticulating Lam, but he wasn't mocking the Samoan – he, too, was angry about something.

After the match, the Samoan camp accused Joost of having called Lam a 'kaffir'. Joost flatly denied the accusation, and when he challenged Lam to repeat his accusation in public – a challenge the Samoan declined to accept – the episode blew over almost as fast as it had erupted. But it certainly was an incident no one wanted to be associated with in the new South Africa.

The Springboks' semi-final opponents were France, whom they were to play at Kings Park in Durban. A problem arose when torrential rains set in. Cancellation of the match would have given victory to the French on the grounds that they hadn't had any players red-carded in the tournament. The situation was starkly simple: because James Dalton and Pieter Hendriks were sent off against Canada in Port Elizabeth, South Africa would be eliminated if the semi-final didn't take place because of rain. (The rain was so bad that, arguably, had the host nation not been involved, there would not even have been a discussion – the match would immediately have been cancelled. But the host nation was involved and badly wanted to win the World Cup, so the game was on.)

There was a crucial moment in the game when the giant French lock Abdelatif Benazzi made an unbelievable surge for the try line, finally being stopped two inches from going over (had he scored, France would have won the match). But for Joost, the most memorable moment of the game was when the selfsame Benazzi tackled him. The pain was indescribable, and Joost soon realised he had broken a rib.

Johan Roux was immediately sent on to replace the injured Van der Westhuizen. At last the game ended and South Africa, by virtue of the 19-15 score, was in the final.

'Fantastic!' Joost thought, except for one thing. 'I knew my rib was cracked. But I couldn't report it to anyone. If I had, they would have dropped me. At that stage not even Kitch, with all his understanding, would have taken a chance on an injured player. And it was non-negotiable – I was going to play in the final.'

In the other semi-final, New Zealand smashed England 45-29 to ensure a dream contest between the old enemies. Such is the respect for the All Blacks in world rugby that, despite the fact that they had had the easier route to the final, they were still strong favourites (16/10) to win the Webb Ellis Trophy. They had won the first World Cup in 1987, but lost it four years later to Australia, so were desperately keen to get their hands on the trophy again. Combined with that burning desire, they had produced the player of the tournament in the powerful wing Jonah Lomu, which conspired to give them an air of invincibility.

Joost solved his broken-rib problem by saying he had bruised the rib *next* to the one that was actually broken. Of course it hurt when the doctor prodded his ribs, but not as badly as it would have had the broken rib been touched. Before each game Joost would have an injection in his 'bruised' rib, which only just made it bearable for him to play.

Apart from Joost's injury, fullback André Joubert's right hand was broken in two places. He had been receiving well-publicised treatment in a decompression chamber and was deemed fit enough to play. 'He was so good,' says Joost, 'that he was probably the only player Kitch would play with an injury.'

Wing James Small was also carrying an injury, but, like Joost, he kept it largely to himself. 'I had a hamstring injury right from the beginning of the tournament,' says Small. 'It happened at the first training session, when I ran into Mark Andrews and hurt my leg. I then pulled my hamstring trying to protect my leg.'

Fortunately for Small, a balance guru called Ron Holder was part of the Springbok set-up (Ron would later work with Arsène Wenger at Arsenal Football Club). 'Without him,' smiles Small, 'I would never have made the final. I missed the game against Canada because of my hamstring.' (Something his mother thinks was the best thing that ever happened, because, she says, he definitely would have got involved in the fighting.)

'But,' says Small, 'besides winning it, I didn't really enjoy the World Cup, as I couldn't perform at my peak. I mean, I never scored a try during the tournament. It was a bit of a disappointment for me ... Mind you, having said that, how could playing in a final like that be a disappointment?'

Apart from the release of Nelson Mandela from Victor Verster Prison on 11 February 1990, the most anticipated day in South Africa's history, Saturday 24 June 1995, dawned sunny and beautifully clear to the palpable excitement of a nation, for once completely united behind *their* Springboks.

Before the game kicked off, in a reprise of the fanatical reception that had greeted him just four weeks earlier at the opening of the World Cup, as the stately President Mandela walked onto the field to be introduced to the players, the Ellis Park faithful rose as one and bellowed, '*Nelson! Nelson! Nelson ...*' as if their very lives depended on it. When the crowd realised that their new president was wearing a Springbok jersey with captain François Pienaar's No. 6 on the back, so loud was the approving, cacophonous roar, it was as if Ellis Park the stadium, like the walls of Jericho, might come tumbling down.

Springbok Kobus Wiese then delighted the expectant supporters when, during the haka, he edged closer and closer to the chanting Kiwis, until he stood nose to nose with the massive Jonah Lomu.

Eventually the game got under way and, exhausted with excitement, the fans finally sat down to watch what, unbeknown to them, was to be South Africa's all-time finest sporting hour ...

The match started off in predictable fashion with neither side giving any quarter. There were no sweeping moves, just grim defence and a few attacking probes. Eventually something had to give, and the Kiwis scored first with a penalty by Andrew Mehrtens, the irritatingly accurate All Black flyhalf. However, Springbok flyhalf Joel Stransky soon replied with a penalty kick of his own.

Another penalty apiece, and the score after 20 minutes was tied at 6-6.

After 30 minutes it was 9-6 in the Springboks' favour, after the ever-reliable Joel Stransky landed a drop goal.

The Kiwis' ace in the pack, giant winger Jonah Lomu, was surprisingly quiet until about 10 minutes into the second half, when he finally broke the first line of the Springboks' defence and, like a rampaging bull, headed for the try line. However, before he had gone 15 metres, Joost van der Westhuizen tackled him head-on to bring the colossus down in an immobile heap.

'We were so ready,' smiles Joost. 'We would have tackled each other for a chance to get at him. My job was to look after Mehrtens and, as cross-defence, to go after Lomu. When I saw Mehrtens giving an inside pass to him, I realised I had two choices. My name was either going to be Michael Catt for the rest of my life, or I was going to take him out. [Lomu had run straight over Michael Catt in the semi-final against England.] I took him out.'

When Springbok flank Ruben Kruger burst over the All Black try line from close range, it looked as if the match was swinging South Africa's way. But the referee, Ed Morrison, disallowed the touchdown. With the teams matching each other score for score, Mehrtens then kicked a drop goal: score 9-9.

With three minutes remaining, the All Blacks were awarded a scrum close to the Springbok line. Joost guessed they would go for a drop goal. As the ball was fed to All Black flyhalf Mehrtens, Joost charged him as fast as he had ever tried to close down a flyhalf, his hands raised to block the kick. He missed. So did Mehrtens.

Extra time. Around the stadium, thousands of visibly exhausted supporters stood in virtual silence as they contemplated the next 30 most important minutes in the history of South Africa ... Africa ... the world ... the universe? Whatever, it was going to be *very* important.

In the first half of extra time, Mehrtens' third penalty of the day subdued even the hardiest of souls watching the epic battle. However, every South African's favourite Jew (in South African rugby folklore, it is considered good luck to have a Jew in the side), Joel Stransky, slotted his third penalty on the stroke of half-time to level the score at 12-12.

The game became a war of attrition as tired pack desperately fought tired pack for the elusive ball. Finally, with about six minutes remaining, South Africa was awarded a scrum near the All Blacks' try line, to the right of the posts. The ball emerged, and in one movement Joost collected and passed it to the waiting Stransky, who kicked *the* most famous drop kick of all time.

Interview with Joel Stransky

In your career you only did three drop goals for the Springboks; tell me about that?
Yes – two in the final and one in the opening game of the World Cup. And the first one was right bang in front. Kobus [Wiese] could have kicked it. But interestingly, in our last warm-up game before the World Cup we played against Western Province at Newlands, as an SA XV, and we beat them in the last minute – by a drop kick! And not the easiest one either; it was a bit from the side and there was a lot of pressure. Then after the opening game against Australia, when there was nothing else on and I popped it over, Kitch Christie [coach] planted the seed when he said, 'Why don't you kick more drop kicks?' And if you are a natural kicker of the ball as flyhalf, the drop kick is in your armoury.

George Foreman says that the final uppercut that put Frazier down for the sixth and final time and won him the World Heavy Weight Title defined his life and almost became an albatross around his neck. How has the winning drop goal in the 1995 Rugby World Cup defined your life?
I understand exactly what George Foreman is saying, but it depends on how you look at it. There are not many people who are fortunate to have ONE absolutely monumental, defining moment behind them.

> They may have some big moments and some great moments, but to have one momentous defining moment is a great honour – and it's nice to be recognised for it; but I do understand what he is saying because I would like to be remembered as more than just a one-drop flyhalf. In many people's eyes, that was all it was – there was actually so much more to it. If you have to describe me as a rugger player, drop kicks would not be in the description (laughs).
>
> *The Weekender*, 1–2 November 2008

The next few minutes were the longest and most agonising of the new South Africa's brief history. But finally referee Ed Morrison blew his whistle to bring the 1995 World Cup to an end and officially confirm South Africa as the new holder of the Webb Ellis Trophy: South Africa 15, New Zealand 12.

'It's hard to remember how I felt when the final whistle blew,' says Joost, 'as there was just so much excitement both on and off the field. There was happy chaos everywhere, as well as relief. But it was unforgettable walking the lap of honour around the pitch, carrying the trophy and seeing how happy we had made every-body. At the time I wished it could go on forever. Everything I had ever dreamt of in my rugby career had come together in that moment. I remember holding the trophy and kissing it, and then passing it to others and it coming back to me. Unless you have personally experienced something similar – and very few people are privileged to have such a magical moment – it really is hard to explain just how wonderful it feels.'

On the field, a reporter said to Springbok captain François Pienaar that 'there were 65 000 South Africans [at Ellis Park] today'.

'We didn't have 65 000 South Africans here today; we had 43 million South Africans,' was François' classic response.

'People have said that the All Blacks were the stronger side,' Joost reflects, 'and it would be hard to argue with that. They had been together for a longer period, and man for man they probably outpowered us, but they could not match our shared resolve. That is why we won the World Cup – because Morné du Plessis and Kitch Christie took a squad of rugby players and turned them into a family who played for each other. We shared everything as a squad and, most importantly, we shared a belief that this was a tournament for us to win. It was our moment, and we were proved right.

'There is no doubt that it was the greatest moment of my career. In fact, I could play through 50 rugby careers and never know a moment quite like the day we won the World Cup in 1995, before our own fans, at a time when rugby was pulling the country together as never before or since' (*Joost: For Love and Money* by Edward Griffiths).

President Nelson Mandela, still wearing the No. 6 Springbok jersey, presented the trophy to François Pienaar. 'Thank you for what you have done for South Africa,' he congratulated the weary Springbok captain.

'We could never do what you have done for South Africa,' Pienaar replied humbly.

The 1995 World Cup turned out to be one of the significant achievements in cementing and augmenting the new South Africa's nascent democracy. It went far beyond what even the most positive of social commentators could ever have predicted. In 2007, South Africa would win the Webb Ellis Trophy a second time, but never again would the Rugby World Cup be as important to every South African as it was on that late, sunny Saturday afternoon of 24 June 1995.

Postscript

After the 1995 World Cup final, there were rumours that the All Blacks had been poisoned just before the big game. Years later All Black captain Sean Fitzpatrick said the following in an interview:

I suppose the question is inevitable – but do you think the All Blacks were poisoned before the World Cup final in 1995?
There was definitely food poisoning – whether it was on purpose or not we will never know. I can remember Louis Luyt, who had always been very good to us, saying, 'Sean, all I want is for South Africa to play the All Blacks in the final and I'll do everything I can to make it happen.' We were looked after like you can't believe; no phone calls during the night; no noise in our hotel area; it was wonderful – until we were in the final.

Suddenly the odd car alarm would go off during the night; stupid phone calls would come in – wrong numbers, that sort of thing; in hindsight we should have got out of Johannesburg and gone somewhere on our own. Anyway, up until then we'd been eating in the hotel restaurant with the other guests, but on the Thursday before the game we thought we'd have lunch on our own.

Friday morning there were 16 of the 21 guys down and out. To be realistic, there were a lot of things we didn't deal with well. We didn't handle the Jonah Lomu thing properly. From a good player, suddenly he was a superstar – we should have used him as a decoy. Instead we kept shovelling the ball to him. Also, we were a young team. We were a bit naive, and physically we weren't really strong enough. There was also the whole Mandela buzz, just the whole amazing occasion. It's impossible to blame one thing.

The Weekender, 29–30 November 2008

Postscript 2

World Cup champion and Springbok lock forward Kobus Wiese had a slightly different take on what had transpired:

I think it was a matter of the All Blacks being devastated. They came as the outright favourites to South Africa. They believed 100% they were going to win the World Cup, but then it didn't go their way – so they were blown completely out of the water. I believe it was only a story because nobody else but the team members got sick from the food at the hotel – so what are the chances that they got poisoned and no one else? It's absolute crap.

The Weekender, 18–19 October 2008

Postscript 3

World Cup champion Hennie le Roux:

Jumping to the final of the 1995 World Cup – the stories about the All Blacks being poisoned or having food poisoning; what's your take on that?
It would be nice if that story was buried once and for all. But I heard rumours that some of the All Blacks had walked to town the day before the final and they ate chilli dogs or something. That could have made them ill. But at the end of the day, that game should have been over in 80 minutes, because Ruben Kruger scored a legitimate try that was disallowed. I sincerely hope that there wasn't any underhand stuff – I don't believe there was.

The Weekender, 23–24 May 2009

11

Professionalism

During the 1995 World Cup, rugby finally turned professional. Joost was one of the more junior players, so he wasn't much caught up in all the wheeling and dealing that was going on behind the scenes. He tended to go with the flow of his fellow Springbok squad members.

In his book *The Rugby War*, Peter FitzSimons opens by saying, 'Whenever a definitive history of the Rugby Union game is written, 1995 will forever stand out as a seminal year of extraordinary change.

'After the code had lived on a diet of fresh air and love for well over a century, it was the year that three national Rugby Unions of the southern hemisphere signed a deal with a massive media corporation guaranteeing them over half a billion American dollars in return for a decade's worth of television rights.

'In reply, an organisation called the World Rugby Corporation (WRC) launched a stunning counter-coup, contracting most of the planet's best players from all the major Unions to an alternative competition set up on a *global* basis.'

Most of the behind-the-scenes to-ing and fro-ing went unnoticed by the press and, hence, the rugby-loving public. In South Africa, Springbok captain François Pienaar emerged as one of the major 'players' in the negotiations. He had a huge influence on the other Springboks' ultimate decision not to sign with the WRC.

After a complicated round of discussions on different continents between a wide range of interested parties, and not without some consummate skulduggery on both sides, the players decided as a body to sign with their respective unions.

Edward Griffiths in *Joost: For Love and Money*, says, 'Amid a rush of secret meetings and deals, South African rugby lost its innocence. The players were understandably seeking to cash in on their moment of glory; the officials were striving to keep the books balanced. Decency dissolved.'

FitzSimons sums it up thus: 'When the war was over, the International Rugby Board – nominally the game's ruling body, even if missing in action throughout – formalised the already apparent. They announced that the code would henceforth abandon its famous amateur ethos and instead embrace outright professionalism.'

Around this time, Joost was also receiving offers from Rugby League agents to switch to their code. The Sydney Bulldogs put in a big play for his services by offering him upwards of R3 million for a two-year contract. Eventually the chief executive of the Bulldogs, Peter Moore, flew out to South Africa to try to convince the obstinate world-class scrumhalf to accept the generous offer. All to no avail.

The English Rugby League club Leeds was also trying to engage Joost's services, but after talking to former Springbok wing Ray Mordt, who had spent the last two years of his career playing for league club Wigan, Joost decided to drop the idea of leaving South Africa and changing codes.

Interview with Ray Mordt

And then you went and played rugby league for Wigan?
Well, I'd given my life to rugby and I had nothing to show for it. I never had any assets – I never had a house, or anything. And I was offered huge money, £100 000 to go and play Rugby League. So Rob Louw and I went – but when we got over there, it wasn't all kosher. In the end I had to get us 'sold'; we got £65 000 for three years – big difference! But I needed to do something with my life. I had my first daughter and life without money was getting difficult.

> **What was the rugby like?**
> It was very different, although I really enjoyed it. The defence and the tackling were tough – there were more big hits. It's very aggressive too. It was also quite hard because they had a Kiwi coach who didn't like us, because we came from Rugby Union, so we struggled to get as many games as we should. In the end, after about two years, they released Rob [Louw] because he got injured and so I asked if I could get released. They let me go as well and I came back [to South Africa].
>
> *The Weekender,* 22–23 November 2008

The Springboks did actually sign contracts with the WRC, represented by Australian Ross Turnbull and tentatively backed by Kerry Packer. 'It was more of a negotiating tool,' says Joost, 'because at that stage SARFU wasn't talking big money and Turnbull was talking in the millions.'

According to Joost, François Pienaar was the custodian of the WRC contracts that were signed by the entire 1995 Springbok World Cup squad, with the exception of Brendan Venter, the centre. 'I don't think any of us really thought we would join the rebels,' says Joost. 'It was more to give us some bargaining power with SARFU. To be honest, I didn't even read the contract before signing it. We all just signed as a team, and if the rest of the guys were happy, then so was I.'

He laughs. 'I think Brendan was the only player who said he wanted to read the contract first.'

Protracted talks between almost everyone involved followed, and eventually Louis Luyt unilaterally decided to pay the players whatever they had been promised by Turnbull. It was all over bar the shouting.

The Springboks had retained the option to withdraw from the WRC contracts by never actually delivering them. It had been agreed that the contracts would effectively remain only options until physically handed over to Turnbull. On 4 August 1995, most of the Springbok squad involved in the negotiations gathered at the Protea Hotel Midrand to finalise their decision. Cannily, while they met, Pienaar kept the signed WRC contracts in the boot of his car so that they couldn't inadvertently be obtained by Turnbull. It was agreed among the squad that they would all abide by the majority decision.

A show of hands decided the voting. Although the players voted overwhelmingly to sign with SARFU, there were a few abstentions.

Professionalism had arrived, and rugby would never be the same again.

Interview with Joost van der Westhuizen

When you started as an amateur, what were you doing for a living?
I was a student. My career was fifty percent amateur and fifty percent professional. In the beginning I didn't earn a lot. But in 1996 we suddenly got big money.

What was big money?
Well, some guys got between two and four and a half million rand for three-year contracts. But it caused a big rift between the guys who won the World Cup (1995), and the guys who were trying to become Springboks. Money changed the game from a team sport into one for individuals. Players largely play for themselves now.

The Weekender, 21–23 March 2009

Joost doesn't recall much about the meetings that took place mostly behind closed doors, but he does recall one particularly memorable encounter with the supreme negotiator – some would say bully – and president of SARFU, Louis Luyt. It was quite a while after the dust had settled on the WRC–SARFU contest for the players' signatures, although Joost can't put a date to the occasion. The meeting was to discuss contracts and remuneration with the entire Springbok squad.

'Louis arrived with a pile of contracts under his arm,' says Joost, 'and without greeting anyone sat down and said, "What's this meeting all about?"'

'Morné du Plessis [Springbok manager] thanked everyone for coming and then started to explain what we were going to discuss. Suddenly, Louis said, "Whoa ... What's he doing here?" and pointed at Teichmann.'

Apparently, the SARFU president then turned to Morné and said, 'As manager, you should know better. These contracts,' holding a pile of papers aloft, 'have a confidentiality clause in them, and unless things have changed that I don't know about, *he* doesn't have a contract.' Again he pointed at the by-now squirming Teichmann. (As Teichmann had not been part of the 1995 World Cup squad, he didn't have a contract at that stage.)

'Out,' Luyt said. 'He can't listen to our discussions because of the confidentiality clause.' Poor Gary had to leave.

Well, that was the end of any resistance from the players. Before the meeting, they had all made notes of issues they wanted to raise about matters they were unhappy about or thought should change. When Luyt asked if anyone had anything to say, there was silence. 'I hid my piece of paper under the table,' laughs Joost.

'Luyt was hugely impressive,' he says. 'The way he walked in with all the contracts under his arm, shutting Morné up and sending Gary out ... That meeting was done and dusted in 10 minutes, and we never got a thing out of it.'

Interview with Ray Mordt

What was your relationship with Dr Luyt like?
You know, I once had to go see him about a problem. So I went to his office and asked his secretary Susanne if I could see him. She

said he was busy, but I said, 'I need to see him.' I was nervous –
going to see Doc was like going to see the headmaster. Eventually
she says you can go in. I went in, and he was sitting there with a
face like thunder. I was a bit flustered and very anxious and just
blurted out, 'What's wrong? Why are you so uptight?' and I started
laughing nervously. At first he just scowled and then he also cracked
up, laughing with me. We discussed whatever we had to, and we
went for lunch. So we got on great. I'm very fond of him – there
were certain things I wished I had more backing in, but I left on
good terms. Before I got a fax (laughs).

The Weekender, 22–23 November 2008

It seems Louis Luyt caused apprehension in even the bravest of
the Springboks.

12

André Markgraaff

Remembered largely for the wrong reasons, André Markgraaff's tenure as Springbok coach came to a premature, tearful and apologetic end. In a meeting with André Bester, his former Griquas captain, Markgraaff had referred to black administrators as 'kaffirs'. What he didn't know, but soon found out, was that Bester had recorded their conversation and would later release the damning tape to the press.

Joost gets quite animated when he talks about the incident. 'It is just another example of how Afrikaners bring their own down,' he says, glossing over the fact that Markgraaff had displayed a nasty, patronising racism in his comments.

At the time, Joost van der Westhuizen was one of the very few Springboks who phoned Markgraaff and asked him not to resign.

André Markgraaff is also remembered for sacking 1995 World Cup–winning captain François Pienaar. At a time when Pienaar was recognised as the unsurpassed captain in world rugby, Markgraaff not only ruthlessly dumped him, but did so without informing François in person.

However, according to Joost, Markgraaff was a great coach. 'He had rugby in his blood. He was very direct and put a lot of trust in his players. He actually spoke to his players and discussed their games with them – something Ian Mac only seemed to do with the senior players. And I suppose because Markgraaff was Afrikaans-speaking, I understood him better.'

After each match, Markgraaff would give each player a written report on his game, which the players really appreciated, says Joost. 'We all loved the feedback.'

Year	Vs	Score	Scrumhalf	Flyhalf	Captain	Tries
1996		**SA-Other**				
	Fiji	43-18	Joost	Henry Honiball	François Pienaar	
	Australia	16-21	Joost	Henry Honiball	François Pienaar	
	New Zealand	11-15	Johan Roux	Joel Stransky	François Pienaar	
	Australia	25-19	Johan Roux	Joel Stransky	François Pienaar	
	New Zealand	18-29	Joost	Joel Stransky	François Pienaar	
	New Zealand	19-23	Johan Roux	Joel Stransky	Gary Teichmann	
	New Zealand	26-33	Joost	Joel Stransky	Gary Teichmann	1
	New Zealand	32-22	Joost	Henry Honiball	Gary Teichmann	2
	Argentina	46-15	Joost	Henry Honiball	Gary Teichmann	1
	Argentina	44-21	Joost	Henry Honiball	Gary Teichmann	
	France	22 -12	Joost	Henry Honiball	Gary Teichmann	
	France	13-12	Joost	Henry Honiball	Gary Teichmann	
	Wales	37-20	Joost	Henry Honiball	Gary Teichmann	3
Tests: won 8, lost 5						

Markgraaff had some of Kitch Christie's more cunning ways. 'After we'd won two games against Argentina and one match against France, he said that if we beat France in the next test, we wouldn't have to train for the last game against Wales. Well, we beat France and then travelled to Wales. When we got there,

Teichmann said no, we needed to train, so he went to Markgraaff and told him the players wanted a practice. André just smiled. Of course it had been his plan all along that we would train – he just wanted to check the team's commitment.'

According to Joost, 'he was an open coach, always there for the players. For example, he always made sure we had a table-tennis table or a pool table in the team room so that the guys could relax when they had time off. He would also allocate the better airline seats to the senior and bigger players. Often, when there weren't enough seats in first or business class, he would end up in economy. With him the players always came first, before management.'

It was under Markgraaff that Joost got to know Sharks flyhalf Henry Honiball. Joost had played one game with the elusive No. 10 and a few provincial games against him, but had never really properly made his acquaintance. It was only when Honiball became Markgraaff's regular flyhalf, at the expense of the injured Stransky, that Joost had the chance to find out what he was really like. In the next couple of years, they would partner each other 24 times at international level.

'He was a hard player,' says Joost. 'In 1996, Northern Transvaal played the Sharks at Kings Park. I went around the scrum and threw a perfect dummy that everyone, including my team, fell for – everyone, that is, except Honiball. His tackle was the hardest anyone ever made on me in my rugby career. He hit me so hard he cracked my sternum.'

At last Joost had met someone who was even quieter than him. 'We called him "Spook", because he just floated around; you never heard him. Even when he tackled me so hard, he never said a word. He just smiled.'

Henry Honiball was more generally known to the public as 'Lem', meaning 'blade', because he could slice through opposition teams seemingly at will; conversely, he would mow them down if they had the temerity to run at him.

'I once asked him how come his tackles were so lethal,' says Joost. 'Henry said he would watch the feet of the player he was tackling and when both were in the air and thus had the least traction, he would bring him down.

'During 1996, with Henry on the outside and André Venter on my inside, no attack ever got through the three of us,' observes Joost. 'We were a brilliant combination, even if I say so myself. Later, when Mallett dropped Venter for Skinstad, it was the beginning of the team's decline.'

Joost also notes that Markgraaff was a good motivator and tactician. And, he points out: 'It was the first time we had an Afrikaans coach, Markgraaff, and an English captain, Teichmann, and it worked surprisingly well. They were very different, but they worked very well together.'

According to Joost, Markgraaff was the first coach who used 'smart' tactics. 'I don't want to call them *skelm* – "smart" sounds better,' he says, smiling. 'For instance, Markgraaff knew the French were good scrummagers. So when we went down to scrum, we would take a step back, which made it look as if the French had pushed too early, and we would get a penalty,' he laughs.

'But the problem with him, as well as with Carel du Plessis (Markgraaff's successor), was that they were amateurs in what had just become a professional world.'

In 1998, Markgraaff took Griqualand West to the semi-finals of the Currie Cup. In 2000 he rejoined SARFU as assistant coach to Harry Viljoen, and at last count was still with SARU. (The South African Rugby Football Union (SARFU) became the South African Rugby Union (SARU) in 2005.)

13

Carel du Plessis

Carel du Plessis was known as the 'Prince of Wings' when he played for the Springboks. Unfortunately, he was never the prince of coaches. After a resounding defeat of Tonga, he went straight into a losing series against the touring British Lions. He was roundly pilloried for not having gone into the matches with a dedicated kicker. 'However,' says Joost, 'that is unfair criticism. He was coming from an amateur background and expected that the guys who were supposed to be able to kick, like Henry [Honiball]

Year	Vs	Score	Scrumhalf	Flyhalf	Captain	Tries
1997		SA-Other				
	Tonga	74-10	Joost	Henry Honiball	Gary Teichmann	1
	Britain	16-25	Joost	Henry Honiball	Gary Teichmann	
	Britain	15-18	Joost	Henry Honiball	Gary Teichmann	1
	Britain	35-16	Joost	Jannie de Beer	Gary Teichmann	1
	New Zealand	32-35	Joost	Jannie de Beer	Gary Teichmann	
	Australia	20-32	Joost	Jannie de Beer	Gary Teichmann	
	New Zealand	35-55	Joost	Jannie de Beer	Gary Teichmann	1
	Australia	61-22	Joost	Jannie de Beer	Gary Teichmann	
Tests: won 3, lost 5						

and Jannie [de Beer], would be able to kick reliably. Nowadays it wouldn't be left to chance, as they would have a kicking coach – and a scrumhalf coach, a mental coach, etc. But Carel hadn't caught up with the new professional game yet. I think the system let him down. The game had also evolved from when he had played.'

According to Joost, when Du Plessis introduced Jannie de Beer into the Springbok team as a specialised kicker in the third and final test against the British Lions and he didn't perform too well, Jannie also realised he had to become more professional. 'And he did. Look what Jannie did to England in the quarter-final of the 1999 World Cup. Five drop goals – I think it is still a record.'

Joost smiles as he remembers the third test against the Lions, 'and I *hate* to remember this, but Matt Dawson threw a dummy that Gary Teichmann and I fell for hook, line and sinker. He held on to the ball and ran across and scored a try in the corner. The players were very disappointed to lose the series to the Lions. I mean, it's a once-off in your career, and we blew it.'

One of the problems was that every time a new coach started, the players had to get used to his ideas for the game. 'For instance,' Joost points out, 'André Markgraaff had come out of a forward background, so he tended to focus on that area of play. Carel came out of a backline background, so he was intent on the Springboks playing an expansive, running game.'

He also feels that the English-speaking Springboks might have had some difficulty understanding Du Plessis' ideas, just as he had struggled a little with Ian McIntosh. 'The irony is that when it all did come together for Carel, after what was to be his last test (a 61-22 thrashing of Australia), he was fired.'

It was a difficult period for Springbok rugby. Although the game had turned professional, nothing had really changed except for the fact that the players were now openly paid. However, a gradual awareness took hold that the New Zealanders were well advanced in adapting to the new order and that the Australians weren't far behind. It was thus imperative that South African rugby got its act together.

14

Nick Mallett

With the appointment of Nick Mallett, it was back to an English coach for Joost. 'I was quite apprehensive,' he says, 'because I hadn't met him. All I knew about him was that he was very strict. With him it was "my way or the highway".'

In the beginning, the new man got on the scrumhalf's case, continually telling him he must communicate. 'Talk to your forwards, talk to your flyhalf … communicate, communicate!' was Mallett's constant refrain. And it irritated Joost.

'If I look back, I shouldn't have taken it as personally as I did. Early on, Nick called all the Afrikaans guys together and explained that he was passionate about rugby and we mustn't take the things he said about us personally. I should have listened, but I don't think I was a good listener.' Although he does admit that, from then on, matters did improve.

Year	Vs	Score	Scrumhalf	Flyhalf	Captain	Tries
1997		SA-Other				
	Italy	62-31	Joost	Henry Honiball	Gary Teichmann	
	France	36-32	Joost	Henry Honiball	Gary Teichmann	
	France	52-10	Werner Swanepoel	Henry Honiball	Gary Teichmann	
	England	29 -11	Werner Swanepoel	Henry Honiball	Gary Teichmann	
	Scotland	68-10	Werner Swanepoel	Henry Honiball	Gary Teichmann	

Year	Vs	Score	Scrumhalf	Flyhalf	Captain	Tries
1998		**SA-Other**				
	Ireland	37-13	Joost	Gaffie du Toit	Gary Teichmann	
	Ireland	33-0	Joost	Franco Smith	Gary Teichmann	1
	Wales	96-13	Joost	Franco Smith	Gary Teichmann	1
	England	18-0	Joost	Henry Honiball	Gary Teichmann	1
	Australia	14-13	Joost	Henry Honiball	Gary Teichmann	1
	New Zealand	13-3	Joost	Henry Honiball	Gary Teichmann	
	New Zealand	24-23	Joost	Henry Honiball	Gary Teichmann	1
	Australia	29-15	Joost	Henry Honiball	Gary Teichmann	
	Wales	28-20	Joost	Henry Honiball	Gary Teichmann	1
	Scotland	35-10	Joost	Henry Honiball	Gary Teichmann	1
	Ireland	27-13	Joost	Henry Honiball	Gary Teichmann	1
	England	7-13	Joost	Henry Honiball	Gary Teichmann	
1999						
	Italy	74-3	Werner Swanepoel	Gaffie du Toit	Gary Teichmann	
	Italy	101-0	Dave von Hoesslin	Gaffie du Toit	Corné Krige	
	Wales	19-29	Werner Swanepoel	Braam van Straaten	Gary Teichmann	
	New Zealand	0-28	Dave von Hoesslin	Gaffie du Toit	Gary Teichmann	
	Australia	6-32	Werner Swanepoel	Braam van Straaten	Rassie Erasmus	

Year	Vs	Score	Scrumhalf	Flyhalf	Captain	Tries
1999		SA-Other				
	New Zealand	18-34	Joost	Gaffie du Toit	Joost	1
	Australia	10-9	Joost	Jannie de Beer	Joost	
	Scotland	46-29	Joost	Jannie de Beer	Joost	1
	Spain	47-3	Werner Swanepoel	Jannie de Beer	André Vos	
	Uruguay	39-3	Joost	Jannie de Beer	Joost	1
	England	44-21	Joost	Jannie de Beer	Joost	1
	Australia	21-27	Joost	Jannie de Beer	Joost	
	New Zealand	22-18	Joost	Henry Honiball	Joost	
2000						
	Canada	51-18	Joost	Braam van Straaten	André Vos	
	England	18-13	Joost	Braam van Straaten	André Vos	
	England	22-27	Joost	Braam van Straaten	André Vos	1
	Australia	23-44	Werner Swanepoel	Louis Koen	André Vos	
	New Zealand	12-25	Werner Swanepoel	Braam van Straaten	André Vos	
	Australia	6 -26	Werner Swanepoel	Braam van Straaten	André Vos	
	New Zealand	46-40	Werner Swanepoel	Braam van Straaten	André Vos	
	Australia	18-19	Werner Swanepoel	Braam van Straaten	André Vos	
Tests: won 27, lost 11						

Joost interrupts his rugby reveries to tell a story that happened off the field. In 1997, Joost's older brother Pieter was an officer in the South African police force. At the time he was in the squad-car division, patrolling the East Rand, and he would often regale the family with stories of his escapades. One night, after relating his latest adventure, Joost expressed an interest in accompanying him on a patrol some time.

Not long afterwards, Pieter arranged to collect Joost on a Friday night from their father's house. When Pieter arrived, he gave Joost a bullet-proof jacket and told him to sit in the back of the patrol car. They headed off towards the highway in the direction of Johannesburg airport.

After cruising around for a couple of hours with not much happening, a message came over the radio at about 11 p.m. instructing them to go to a nearby farm, where it was suspected an arms cache was being unloaded.

With blue light flashing and siren blaring, they raced down the Olifantsfontein off-ramp towards the farm. Joost hung on for dear life in the back of the car, where he had been dozing. Suddenly he was wide awake.

When they were still a few kilometres from the farm, they turned off the siren, the blue light and the car's headlights. As they slowed down to almost a crawl, Joost had the nasty feeling that they might be heading into an ambush.

'Listen, boys,' he said, 'I know this isn't my game, but you're going into a farm in the dark, alone. Don't you want to call for some back-up?' He didn't want to sound as if he was scared, but the situation didn't look good to him.

Pieter and his partner just ignored Joost as they got their guns out and scanned the road ahead.

'Guys,' Joost tried again, 'don't you think this is the perfect setting for an ambush?' As he said 'ambush', all hell broke loose.

A fusillade of shots went off somewhere to the right of the squad car. Pieter immediately braked and returned fire. Meanwhile, his partner jumped out of the vehicle and raced towards the bushes where the shots had come from, firing his gun as he ran. Joost couldn't believe what was going on and ducked as low as he could in the back of the car. After what seemed an absolute age, the firing stopped. There was an eerie silence. As another sudden burst of firing broke out, Pieter yelled, 'Joost, are you okay?'

'Yes,' Joost replied, 'I'm okay, but just give me a bloody gun!'

Again there was silence, which went on for quite a few minutes. Joost slowly raised his head to see what was going on and, to his absolute amazement, saw about seven smiling policemen staring into the car. The whole thing had been a set-up.

'I'll get you guys one day,' he smiled at them. 'I'll get you.'

With the advent of professionalism, the game was evolving quicker than it ever had before, and the scrumhalf found he was performing more of a link than an offensive role. This ran counter to his naturally predatory, attacking game. Under Nick Mallett he had to adapt to no longer 'breaking', because, as Mallett kept pointing out, in doing so he ran away from his support. (Which of course begs the question: Should he have run *towards* his support?)

But not everything was serious with Nick. One day some of the players conspired to put a sleeping pill in the coach's coffee. The bus ride to that day's practice field was about 40-odd minutes long, and Nick slept the whole way. To the sleeping-pill dispensers' horror, a large contingent of the French press was waiting to interview Mallett about the forthcoming test match when the bus arrived at the rugby fields.

Although he felt a bit wobbly and drowsy from his little siesta, Mallett happily went to chat to them, in French, as was his habit. The problem was, he sounded as if he was drunk. He couldn't seem to pronounce his words properly and had difficulty sticking to a particular train of thought.

The French pressmen were delighted, thinking they had a scoop. Fortunately, before any of them could head off to spread news of *le scandal*, the conspirators intercepted them and explained why Mallett was not his normal eloquent and loquacious self.

Mallett was, of course, furious about the incident and had a complete sense-of-humour failure. Joost says that they felt the backlash of the coach's ire during the following week's training sessions.

At the end of 1998, on 5 December, Joost played his 50th test for the Springboks against England at Twickenham. He proudly flew his parents over to watch the match. It was the first time his mother had been overseas. 'Also the last time,' he says, laughing. When asked how she'd enjoyed the trip, Joost smiles and says, 'You'll have to ask her.' The whole exercise was a huge disappointment, as South Africa lost 7-13 and, after an indifferent display, Joost also badly injured his knee.

After losing 0-28 to New Zealand, Nick Mallett, to the ire of virtually all South African rugby fans, dropped the Springbok captain Gary Teichmann before the 1999 World Cup. He based his decision on the principle that a captain must always be assured of his place in a side. According to Mallett, Gary was no longer the first-option No. 8 for the Springboks, so he therefore had no choice but to relieve him of the captaincy.

In his book *For the Record*, Teichmann graphically presents his version of events:'On Friday morning, I called again, left another message in his voicemail and, two hours later, around 11 o'clock, the Springbok coach came on the line. It was the first time he had called me in three months, and I happened to be lying in the physiotherapy room at Kings Park, having treatment.

'"Gary?"

'"Yes."

'"I have decided to change the captain for the rest of the Tri-Nations series. I don't think you can hold down a place in the team any more, and I suggest you go back to the Natal team and play in the Currie Cup."

'"But Nick, if I may say so, I played pretty well in the second half against Wales and I was Man of the Match against the All Blacks."

"'Look, Gary, that's my decision."

'There was evidently no opportunity for discussion. The pragmatic coach of 1997 had become the absolute ruler of 1999.'

Towards the end of Mallett's tenure as coach, he began using Werner Swanepoel as his starting scrumhalf. As a team player, Joost quite happily sat on the bench until required – at least initially. But as he realised he was gradually being forced out, he confronted Mallett, who just kept saying that 'Smiley' (Swanepoel) was playing well and he didn't really want to drop him.

Joost wasn't alone in feeling that he was being squeezed out. Breyton Paulse, the mercurial Springbok wing, also had a few problems with Mallett.

Interview with Breyton Paulse

Back to rugby; Nick Mallett used to leave you out of the Springbok team, ostensibly because you were small. What was your relationship with him like?

It was a bit dodgy at times. Nick was a chap who preferred big, staunch guys. It was really difficult for me. At the time I was the top try scorer in Super 14, I was playing well and I thought I was at the level where I deserved a chance; but I also kept the team's interests in mind. Although I wasn't going to lie down and let it break me. I just waited for my chance. And then fortunately in that game against the All Blacks I had an opportunity to prove a point and I scored the try that won the game; which was very satisfying, because I think in a way it showed him he was wrong.

The Weekender, 7–8 March 2009

Mallett was eventually ousted as coach when, in a conversation that took place in Durban just before the last Tri-Nations match of 2000, he told a reporter that he thought the price of test tickets was too high. His comments shouldn't have raised eyebrows at SARFU, as they knew how outspoken Mallett was, and usually about issues that were far more important to South African rugby. But it appears as if the men who ran rugby were just looking for a reason to get rid of him. Mallett appeared before a disciplinary panel and was told that he no longer had SARFU's support. A severance package was negotiated, and Mallett was gone.

15

Flying …

The year 1999 started with Joost trying to rehabilitate the knee he had injured against England. Life with a crooked knee proved to be boring; after a week or two of twiddling his thumbs, Joost reviewed his goals and decided he was going to learn to fly. And so one morning he took himself off to Wonderboom Airport and joined a flying school.

He began his instruction with a pilot called Basie van der Bardt, who by all accounts was impressively competent.

Joost was a diligent pupil and thoroughly enjoyed his time with Basie while they circled the airfield, doing what is known in flying vernacular as 'circuits and bumps' – continual landings and take-offs. The main objective was to make an equal number of both and hopefully be able to use the aircraft again.

One morning, as they taxied back to the apron, Basie unexpectedly opened the door of the aircraft and got out.

'Hey, *waar gaan jy*?' the surprised learner pilot inquired.

'I want you to go solo,' Basie said without much emotion. 'Don't worry, I'll be watching,' and he firmly closed the aircraft's door.

'I nearly shat myself,' declares Joost eloquently. 'At that point I only had about 15 hours' flying time.'

Before he could argue, the tower instructed Joost through his headphones to line up and take off. It had had to come, of course – he had naively assumed that there might have been a bit of warning and discussion before the fateful moment.

As the little Cessna lifted into the air, Joost experienced the freedom and excitement every first-time solo pilot feels. He describes the sensation as being one of 'pure success'. The problem was, take-offs were easy – he still had to land … on his own.

'I was sweating, I tell you. I was sweating.'

Fortunately, Basie had taught him well. Before Joost knew it he was safely back on the ground, being congratulated by all and sundry. 'It's just like rugby,' he thought, and basked in the admiration.

Tragically, only two weeks after Joost went solo, Basie was killed when his aeroplane flipped while taking off with a pupil at Wonderboom Airport. Although Joost felt desperately sad and shocked, as he had got to know the always charming instructor well, he carried on his instruction with Jannie Loutzis.

A few weeks later, as part of his final navigational exam, Joost had to do a cross-country flying exercise. The night before the test, he carefully planned his route and got his mind ready for the early-morning flight.

At 6 a.m. he handed in his flight plan and half an hour later took off. Everything went smoothly as he confidently ticked off the checklist.

At Dwaalboom Airport, Joost did a 'touch and go' and contentedly climbed towards his next stop, which was Pilanesberg Airport. Then, at 2 000 feet, he saw that the fuel gauges were showing 'empty'. He tried to call Johannesburg information, but suddenly found he didn't have any communications. The problem was, between him and his next stop lay the Pilanesberg mountains.

There was no way he was going over the range with empty tanks, as should he be forced to put the aircraft down, he would have nowhere to land. He reduced height to 1 000 feet and flew around it.

Not one to be bothered by trifles, Joost took out his cellphone to call for some advice – but there was no signal.

He continued to the Pilanesberg Airport, where he flew low alongside the runway and waggled his wings to indicate to the tower that he had a problem. While doing so, he noticed a jet on the single runway, readying for take-off. He then tried to set his flaps for landing. They didn't work either.

There was nothing for it but to land. With no comms, no fuel indicated and no flaps, Joost decided he wasn't keen on hanging around in the sky. Fortunately the jet didn't move, and apart from an irate air-traffic controller, who had to leave his tower to admonish Joost and simultaneously ask for an autograph, it all ended without serious incident.

Later it was established that an alternator cable had come loose during his touchdown at Dwaalboom Airport, causing the aeroplane's electrics to fail.

For a learner pilot with not many hours' flying time, the whole experience was a bit trying, but it was the sort of thing on which Joost thrived. He continued to fly.

After a second knee operation, which was as a direct consequence of returning to rugby too soon, Joost signed up with Buzz Bezuidenhout at Rand Airport to learn to fly helicopters. Although he had his fixed-wing pilot's licence, Joost had always wanted to fly choppers. Now, because of his knee injury, he had the time to find out what it was like.

His first solo flight in a helicopter equalled the excitement of his first cross-country experience in a fixed-wing aircraft.

Joost seemed to have an aptitude for what most people would consider to be an impossible exercise in control and coordination. 'We were trying to create a record for hovering,' says Joost. 'Most people only hover at about 13 hours' [flying time] – I was trying at seven hours. Buzz made it easy. He told me to look at the parked aircraft and count their windows. I started counting them and then realised that I was standing still – I was hovering. By not watching the ground, which was the natural tendency, I became one with the helicopter.'

Joost went solo at 15 hours. 'That was hairy in the little Robbie [Robinson R22]. As I lifted off and was going into transition, I heard a very strange noise coming from above me. I then realised the rotors had started coning. My instinct was to land, but there were too many revs and I wasn't using enough power, which was why the blades were coning. The proper thing to do was to pull power and go up.'

Joost first hit the ground, creating a huge dust storm, before realising in the nick of time that he was already in transition. He promptly pulled power and fortunately got himself up and out of danger.

'Luckily, just before I landed, I remembered what I was supposed to be doing, but apparently I'd been very close to killing myself. If I'd landed, the chopper would have flipped. Buzz was very cross with me. He crapped on me for not listening to his instructions.'

Eventually Joost accumulated about 100 hours in helicopters. But then life, in the form of a divorce, a marriage to Amor and the arrival of children, intruded, and he didn't have the time to fly.

16

Rugby World Cup 1999

The 1999 World Rugby Cup will forever be associated with Nick Mallett's decision to drop one of South Africa's best, longest-serving, record-equalling (17 games unbeaten) and most respected Springbok captains, Gary Teichmann. Although Teichmann was struggling with injury and, as a consequence, a lack of match practice, there seemed to be more to his sacking than simply a matter of form.

Gary Teichmann played 42 tests (29 wins, 13 losses), scored six tries for the Springboks and captained them 36 times. Not a shabby record by any means.

Mallett first dropped André Venter for his barely disguised favourite, Bobby Skinstad, who was a controversial selection; then he dropped a bombshell by letting Gary Teichmann go.

Earlier in the year, the Springboks had lost to Wales for the first time in history (19-29). Immediately thereafter they flew to New Zealand, where they proceeded to lose 0-28 against the All Blacks at Dunedin. Unbeknown to anyone, except maybe Mallett, the match would turn out to be Gary Teichmann's last in the green and gold.

For the next game against Australia, the Springboks were led by loose forward Rassie Erasmus. They lost 6-32.

When the team returned home and Nick Mallett announced his decision to relieve the Springbok captain of his position to the press, he summed up the matter by saying, 'A captain has to be an automatic selection in the starting 15 – Gary is not an automatic choice.'

Mallett also announced that Joost van der Westhuizen would

captain the team for the remainder of the Tri-Nations series and the 1999 World Cup.

'Nick phoned me,' says Joost, 'and asked whether I would like to be Springbok captain. I said, "I'll get back to you," and I immediately called Gary and asked him what was going on. He told me he had been dropped, and that was it. So I called Nick back and accepted. But I knew then that Nick was making a mistake.' He adds, 'Not by picking me, but by dropping Gary.'

'What was irritating,' said Gary in an interview with eminent rugby writer Dan Retief, 'was being dropped for a guy who wasn't even playing at the time.' Bobby Skinstad had a much-publicised car accident in which he badly damaged his knee at the same time that Teichmann injured his knee. This was after a mysterious incident in a pub in Cape Town that apparently featured the New Zealand scrumhalf Justin Marshall. Upon hearing of his selection to the team, Bobby Skinstad was more sanguine about the situation, saying, 'I can't regret being picked – I don't do the picking.'

Interview with Bob Skinstad

You appeared to be one of Nick Mallett's favourites – he dropped André Venter for you when many people thought Venter should have played. What was your relationship like with Nick?

My relationship was very good with Nick – he was a very good coach. Although I think he got caught up in the hype around how well the team had done. I do believe he made the wrong decision taking me to the World Cup. But as a player you don't call the coach and say don't pick me over another guy; then you seem to spend the rest of your career apologising for not doing just that (laughs). But at that World Cup we had a very good chance of winning it. There was that incredible last-minute drop kick from the Aussies, which was the only thing between us and a date in the final against an under-strength French team, who had just had a

---

murderous game against the All Blacks. But I was still too young to think for a second that there were people who didn't want me there. Later I became more realistic and cynical.

The Weekender, 2–3 May 2009

At the 1999 World Cup, South Africa found themselves in Pool A along with Scotland, Spain and Uruguay.

The first match, between South Africa and Scotland at Murrayfield, was a cracker. The lead changed five times, and the Springboks were behind going into the last 20 minutes. But then they turned it on and scored four tries without reply, eventually outscoring the Jocks by six tries to four and winning 46-29. Try-scorers for the Springboks were Brendan Venter, Robbie Fleck, Ollie le Roux, Deon Kayser, André Venter and the captain, Joost van der Westhuizen.

It was an auspicious start to South Africa's quest to retain the Webb Ellis Trophy, so memorably won in 1995, especially after all the pre-tournament off-the-field distractions. And given that Scotland were the Five Nations champions, the victory was even more significant.

Next up, South Africa played Spain at Murrayfield. For this game, Werner Swanepoel was at scrumhalf, Joost van der Westhuizen was on the bench and the side was captained by André Vos. Although the Springboks scored seven tries in their 47-3 win over a country better known for its football prowess, they didn't look like world champions.

'There was no atmosphere,' says Joost. 'There could only have been about 5 000 people watching, and after the Scotland match, the game against Spain was an anticlimax.'

Tries were scored by captain André Vos (2), Anton Leonard, Pieter Muller, Bobby Skinstad and Werner Swanepoel. South Africa was also awarded a penalty try. Flyhalf Jannie de Beer slotted six conversions.

Although the Springboks had been expected to win, the players always found it a relief when matches against no-hopers were successfully over and devoid of any devastating underdog victories to spoil the show.

'Games that we were supposed to win were always slightly unpleasant,' says Joost, 'as there was never any real upside to them. If we lost, we were useless, and if we won – well, we were supposed to win, so no one was impressed. And of course the weaker teams would be trying harder than they had ever tried before to beat the mighty Springboks ...'

For their next pool game, against Uruguay, the team travelled to Hampden Park in Glasgow. 'Again there were very few people watching,' says Joost, 'which just tended to put a dampener on proceedings. Combined with the awkward hustling and bustling style of play by the South Americans, it all made for a difficult game.' Compounding a shabby display by the world champions was an incident for which Brendan Venter was sent off. 'I think he went in with the shoulder or he stamped on someone,' says Joost.

After the 1995 World Cup, where they were on the brink of being eliminated due to bad weather, South Africa knew all too well the ramifications of having a player red-carded. (Rule 4 (b) states: 'The winner shall be the team which has had the least number of players ordered from the field throughout the tournament.' This simply means that if two sides play to a draw in extra time or if the game is cancelled due to bad weather, the team with the least red cards in the tournament goes through.) The match was duly won 39-3 by the Springboks. Tries were scored by Robbie Fleck, Deon Kayser, Albert van den Berg and captain Joost van der Westhuizen.

With the onset of the quarter-finals, the World Cup took on a more sombre sense of reality. From then on, there could be no slip-ups, no games lost. The Springboks were drawn to meet England in Paris. (England was in the quarter-finals courtesy of coming second in Pool B by beating Italy 67-7; losing to New

Zealand 16-30; thrashing Tonga 101-10; and then beating Fiji 45-24 in the quarter-final playoffs, all at Twickenham.)

The match in Paris between the northern and southern hemisphere teams will always be remembered for Jannie de Beer's incredible kicking display. He slotted two conversions, five penalties and a mind-boggling five drop goals (a South African record) to score 34 points.

Considering that before the tour he hadn't even been the second-choice flyhalf, it was an amazing performance. A lot of credit has to go to Nick Mallett's careful planning. He developed a simple but effective move whereby the robust centre, Pieter Muller, would cut in from midfield, draw in the tackles of the English loose forwards and then quickly recycle the ball via Van der Westhuizen to De Beer for a drop-goal attempt.

De Beer carried out his part admirably by not missing once.

Amusingly, after the game the Afrikaans-speaking De Beer, with unintended irony, attributed his astonishing performance to 'the hand of God'.

The final score was 44-21 to South Africa. The only try for the Springboks was scored by Joost van der Westhuizen.

The last time the Springboks had played against Australia (at Newlands in Cape Town) they had barely scraped home. South Africa had scored a converted try (Robbie Fleck) and a penalty (Jannie de Beer) against three penalties by Australia (they won 10-9). The captain that day had been Joost van der Westhuizen, so he had no illusions as to the enormity of the task as they converged on a rain-sodden Twickenham in South West London for the semi-final against Australia.

And not only was it raining, but the wind was howling through the stadium. Not a good day for rugby – unless, of course, you played for England.

As expected, given the conditions, the game was a dour and unrelenting struggle, with a try never looking likely from either side. There was one opportunity, when George Gregan, the nuggety Australian scrumhalf, dived into what he thought was a gap but was, in fact, Pieter Rossouw and Joost van der Westhuizen waiting to double-tackle him before he could dot the ball down.

Man of the Match was undoubtedly the elusive Australian centre Tim Horan, who had spent the previous day ill in bed. He gave one of the great displays of centre-three-quarter play before he had to leave the field exhausted – probably more from spending the night racing to the toilet and vomiting than from being persecuted by the South Africans. Springbok flank André Venter, who had given England such a rough time the week before, was run through three times by the hard-running Horan. (Horan was later chosen Man of the Tournament.)

South Africa was trailing by three points well into injury time when referee Derek Bevan awarded the Springboks a penalty 38 metres from the Australian goal. So strong was the wind that Jannie de Beer had to ask Joost van der Westhuizen to hold the ball steady after he'd placed it on the tee. Not allowing either the roaring gale or the prostrate form of his lanky scrumhalf lying next to the ball to distract him, De Beer calmly split the posts to keep South Africa in the World Cup. Score: 21-21.

Extra time loomed. The survivors of the 1995 Springbok World Cup–winning team – Joost van der Westhuizen, Mark Andrews, Os du Randt and Chris Rossouw – experienced an overwhelming feeling of déjà vu.

As the game kicked off again, nothing changed. If anything, the game closed up even more into a dogged, unyielding forward struggle for territory that yielded little on either side. Finally, with the scores still tied on 21-all and only seven minutes left to play, George Gregan passed the ball to flyhalf Stephen Larkham just inside the South African half. Larkham broke South African hearts by kicking an outrageously unlikely but superb drop goal. (Annoyingly for the Springboks, Larkham later reckoned he had never landed a drop goal in senior rugby at any level.)

Jannie de Beer, who just six days earlier had so clinically annihilated England in Paris with his five drop goals, missed four attempts on that cold, wet and windy afternoon at Twickenham (he did, however, kick six penalties).

After Larkham's extraordinary kick and with their resolve finally wilting, the South Africans conceded a penalty, which Australian fullback Matthew Burke (eight penalties) kicked over as the final nail in the South Africans' coffin.

So near and yet so far. If the Springboks had won, they would have had to face a French team who had just come off a hard-fought win against New Zealand. Who knows what would have happened?

As it turned out, South Africa salvaged a small measure of success when they beat New Zealand 22-18 in the playoff for third place. Breyton Paulse scored a try, Henry Honiball kicked a conversion and three penalties, and Percy Montgomery slotted two drop goals.

In the final, Australia went on to beat the French 35-12, with which victory they became the first team to win the Rugby World Cup twice (1991 and 1999), both times away from home. The All Blacks (1987) and the Springboks (1995) were both world champions on home territory, but South Africa would win away from home in France in 2007.

After the tournament, news agency Reuters, in the form of former England flyhalf Rob Andrew and former British Lions captain Willie John McBride, drew up a Dream Team from the players who had participated in the 1999 World Cup. Their scrumhalf was Joost van der Westhuizen.

Rob Andrew described Van der Westhuizen thus: 'I have decided Van der Westhuizen offers that little more than Aussie George Gregan and he deserves to be in the Dream Team. He is quick and strong on the break, has a good service, kicks really well, he's an aggressive defender and, above all, he reads the game superbly.'

The rest of the team was:

Fullback: Matthew Burke (Aus); Wings: Ben Tune (Aus), Jonah Lomu (NZ); Centres: Daniel Herbert (Aus), Tim Horan (Aus); Flyhalf: Andrew Mehrtens (NZ); Hooker: Michael Foley (Aus); Locks: Abdelatif Benazzi (Fra), John Eales captain (Aus); Eighth man: Toutai Kefu (Aus); Flank: Olivier Magne (Fra).

South Africans: Props: Cobus Visagie, Os du Randt; Flank: André Venter.

On returning home, Joost van der Westhuizen found himself confronted by a *Rapport* front-page spread headlined, '*Dit was alles Joost se fout!*' It was all Joost's fault. A few players apparently had gripes about his leadership style and blamed him for the team's bad showing.

One wonders whether to lose in the semi-finals to the eventual winners could reasonably be considered a 'bad showing' …?

17

Harry Viljoen

Harry Viljoen was the eighth coach in the eight years since re-admission, a coach with a backline pedigree and some unusual ideas. Definitely his own man, he had a different way of structuring his coaching team – it was more businesslike. He brought in a whole new way of thinking. For instance, says Joost, instead of working against the media, he brought in a media liaison officer, Mark Keohane.

'Personally, I think that was his biggest mistake. We all new Mark Keohane; he always attacked the side, always had something negative to say about the Springboks, but now suddenly Harry was paying him.'

At this point Joost searches through a pile of papers and produces the most amazing bit of information. It is a typed page titled: 'Extract from a document prepared by Mark Keohane for SA Rugby (the business arm of SARFU) early in 2003, in which he detailed his job description.'

Joost is not sure of the document's provenance, or the various comments scribbled on it, but smilingly says, 'I knew it would come in useful some time.' I presume he means that the document supports his theory that Keohane wasn't on the players' side.

The document reads:

Relative to the 2003 World Cup year, my primary focus should be that of spin-doctoring surrounding the national team. Spin-doctoring, as an art, is a largely untapped medium within South African sport. However, I believe it to be among the most important tools within South African sport, especially rugby which has such a strong social and political association.

After stressing the importance of spin-doctoring in general, the document stresses that:

> Spinning has various degrees, from the basic news-providing to advanced spinning which includes dealing with a crisis, leaks, deliberate misinformation, rapid rebuttal, turning the rumours [sic] mill and manipulation of a media which culminates in unofficial control of the media – something every business-related sports be [sic] and views as paramount to ensure brand development.

The next paragraph is self-congratulatory:

> In the past 18 months there have been numerous examples of my spin-doctoring to avert potential crisis [sic] in South African rugby and I know it took effective spin-doctoring to soften and in some instances manipulate the flow of information that could otherwise have proved potentially embarrassing to SA rugby [sic].

But the part that obviously got Joost's goat (because of the Newport debacle, which will be covered later) was this:

> The pre-empting of Percy Montgomery's wanting to go overseas and other overseas-bound players holding SA rugby [sic] to ransom lead [sic] to the players being seen in a bad light and not SA rugby [sic].

Spin-doctoring, 'as an art', was severely discredited during Tony Blair's tenure as prime minister of the United Kingdom

Harry Viljoen

Year	Vs	Score	Scrumhalf	Flyhalf	Captain	Tries
2000		SA-Other				
	Argentina	37-33	Joost	Percy Montgomery	André Vos	
	Ireland	28-18	Joost	Percy Montgomery	André Vos	1
	Wales	23-13	Joost	Percy Montgomery	André Vos	1
	England	17-25	Joost	Braam van Straaten	André Vos	
2001						
	France	23-32	Joost	Butch James	André Vos	
	France	20-15	Joost	Butch James	André Vos	
	Italy	60-14	Neil de Kock	Percy Montgomery	Bobby Skinstad	
	New Zealand	3-12	Joost	Butch James	Bobby Skinstad	
	Australia	20-15	Joost	Butch James	Bobby Skinstad	
	Australia	14-14	Joost	Butch James	Bobby Skinstad	
	New Zealand	15-26	Joost	Butch James	Bobby Skinstad	
	France	10-20	Joost	Braam van Straaten	Bobby Skinstad	
	Italy	54-26	Joost	Louis Koen	Bobby Skinstad	1
	England	9-29	Joost	Louis Koen	Bobby Skinstad	
	USA	43-20	Deon de Kock	Louis Koen	André Vos	
Tests: won 8, drew 1, lost 6						

(1997–2007), when he made excessive use of Alistair Campbell to 'spin-doctor' a number of unpopular and questionable government decisions, so much so that he was openly called a liar in the English press and was eventually nicknamed Tony *Bliar*.

According to Wikipedia, 'Campbell acquired a reputation as a sinister and Machiavellian figure, and both Blair and Campbell have frequently been criticised or satirised for their allegedly excessive use of "spin" and news management techniques.'

But Keohane's own description of 'advance spinning', which, he says, 'includes dealing with a crisis, leaks, deliberate misinformation, rapid rebuttal, turning the rumours [*sic*] mill and manipulation of a media' is a bit of spin-doctoring in itself. He actually makes it sound as if it is a legitimate practice. Granted, dealing with a 'crisis' or 'leaks', if done honestly, can be a legitimate practice. But 'deliberate misinformation' is nothing more than a disingenuous euphemism for lying.

And 'turning the rumours [*sic*] mill and manipulation of a media'? It is unclear how that can be anything other than a cynical attempt to arrive at a not-entirely-factual or honest outcome.

A few players rated Harry Viljoen for reasons other than rugby. In some respects, Harry was like a father to James Small, and Hennie le Roux was hugely impressed by his business acumen.

Joost approved of the fact that Harry brought back Ian McIntosh to help the team on the technical side.

'He did other things too,' says Joost, 'like bringing in computers on which the guys could study their game. He gave us coaching DVDs to work on at night – he even made us buy the DVDs. I've still got mine. We had to work out moves and game plans on these DVDs, which was great fun.'

Interestingly, in *Springbok Saga*, the only time Joost is shown using a computer, he is playing Solitaire.

It was under Harry that Joost's Newport controversy occurred. Joost's version is as follows: during the Super 12, as it was known then, Joost received an offer from Tony Brown, the owner of Newport club in Wales, to play for them. So Joost went off to Harry to ask for his permission – bearing in mind, says Joost, 'that I wanted to play in three World Cups for the Springboks'.

Harry had no problem with the request. So Joost went over to the UK and signed a contract with Tony Brown.

However, Riaan Oberholzer, who was the CEO of SARFU at the time, had different ideas. On the tour to New Zealand, Joost *en passant* informed him of his plans.

'There's no way you can go,' was Riaan's unexpected response. 'It's against SARFU's constitution. Play for Newport and you will never play for the Springboks again.'

Joost then called Tony Brown in Newport and explained his dilemma. According to him, Tony said, 'No problem. I respect your situation. Don't worry. Of course you must play for your country – I will simply tear up the contract.' That was the end of it as far as Joost was concerned, hugely relieved to be out of a tight spot.

Then Mark Keohane got hold of the story, 'presumably because he was part of SARFU,' says Joost. Suddenly he, Joost van der Westhuizen, was the 'Judas' of South African rugby.

'I would have thought I would have been a Judas for rejecting, not for choosing, my country. Apparently someone in the press had got hold of the Newport manager, who at that stage didn't know what had gone on between me and Tony Brown. This manager said that they had jerseys on which my name had been printed, and of course they would lose money. So without checking with me or, for that matter, Tony Brown, the local press just slammed me as a Judas. I was very pissed off.'

Harry, of course, said it hadn't been Keohane who had leaked the story. 'He thanked me for my decision,' says Joost, 'and said he would pay me R300 000 out of his own pocket as some form of compensation for missing out on playing for Newport. Harry actually gave me a personal cheque for R150 000. Unfortunately he left the Springbok set-up before I ever got the rest,' laughs Joost. 'The irony of the whole thing is that I have never even been to Newport. When I dealt with Tony, I met him in London.'

Another aspect of the incident that still rankles with Joost is that after he was pilloried in the press, players like Robbie Kempson, Percy Montgomery, Bobby Skinstad and Gary Teichmann all went to play for Newport *with* SARFU's approval.

In Harry Viljoen's first game as coach, against Argentina, he banned the Springboks from kicking and they very nearly lost the match. 'He took a more balanced stance on kicking after that,' says Joost. 'Oh, and he also introduced businesslike kit. He brought in suits, so we would travel in Number 1 suits so that we would look more like professional businessmen.'

In what turned out to be his last game as coach in 2001, Harry got SARFU to fly the Springboks' wives and girlfriends over to Houston to watch the test against the USA. Apparently that was at a stage when Joost's marriage to Marlene had begun to 'crumble', as he delicately puts it.

'In the end, it was weird – one day Harry decided he had had enough, and he just walked out.'

18

Divorce and marriage – Marlene and Amor

The failure of Joost's first marriage can probably be explained by saying 'don't get married to your sister'. Joost and Marlene had met at school and so, in effect, did their growing up together. And when Marlene's brother Izak was tragically killed in the car accident in Durban, Joost became Marlene's parents' surrogate son. All these events conspired to imbue their liaison with a filial element beyond that normally engendered in a lovers' relationship.

With Joost's constant absence while on rugby tours – he was spending up to seven months a year away – the combination produced a tasteless cocktail that assured a dismal future. And so it proved to be.

The relationship began to disintegrate gradually. Increasingly they found that all they did was irritate each other. They no longer seemed to have anything in common and had little fun together. Eventually Joost realised that he had to get out of the marriage. Fortunately the couple didn't have any children, so the break-up would affect only them ... and their parents; and their extended families; and the public; and his fellow rugby players; and the press ...

When Marlene joined Joost in America, courtesy of Springbok coach Harry Viljoen, who had invited the players' partners to the last test of the year (against the USA on 1 December 2001; the Springboks won 43-20), things came to a head and the couple decided to separate. As things transpired, it was also Harry Viljoen's last test as Springbok coach.

About a month before the Van der Westhuizens actually parted, Joost fatefully met celebrity guest, Lotto presenter, singer and all-round glamour girl Amor Vittone at the Springboks' annual Player of the Year dinner (partners didn't attend that particular function).

Not for a moment guessing how things would develop, they stood in the foyer of the Sandton Convention Centre and chatted for a while, oblivious to the fact that they were providing grist to the rumour mill. Although it was generally known that it was not all sweetness and light in the Van der Westhuizens' marriage, the press, as usual, were looking for an angle that might 'sex up' the degenerating situation.

So of course, before they could even blink, Joost and Amor, in the pages of various publications, became an item. And of course, according to the Fourth Estate, Amor stole Joost.

Interestingly, Joost was not altogether unhappy about one aspect of the media's questionable coverage. 'I don't think they realised it, but in a way they drove us together. I got a call from Amor's father, Dario, who wanted to know what I, a married man, thought I was doing with his daughter. He had seen the articles and wanted an explanation. So I went to see him to clarify the situation, which of course gave me a reason to see Amor again.'

Joost told Dario that he was in the process of getting divorced – to which the former soccer player curtly responded, 'Sure, that's what everybody says.'

'He later admitted,' says Joost, 'that he was very surprised when I actually did get divorced.'

Joost had never really met a girl who could compete for his interest as his mates could. But unexpectedly, without looking for a partner, he had found a remarkably capable woman who was actually much more fun to be with than his rugby 'family'. Even more incredibly, she didn't know anything about rugby. ('Funny, Marlene knew everything about rugby,' Joost laughs. 'Amor still doesn't really have a clue; she pretends she knows what's going on.') So the new target of his affections didn't fully understand why her suitor generated so much fuss. And he liked the fact that she was famous in her own right, because, having experienced the vagaries of constantly being in the limelight herself, Joost guessed Amor wouldn't mind his life in a goldfish bowl.

Amor had obviously got under his skin. 'You know,' he says, 'you get people who light up a room when they walk in and others who can light up a room just by walking out? Well, she was the walking-in type.'

Joost and Marlene were divorced on 17 January 2002. Interestingly, it was a Thursday and not a Friday, the day on which divorces are normally finalised. Joost had found out that the press had been tipped off about the divorce and would be waiting for him at court on the Friday. Fortunately his attorney managed to get the case scheduled for a day earlier.

Telling Marlene that she could keep the house and her car, Joost, clutching a suitcase in each hand, walked to his double cab, climbed in and, for the last time, drove away from the five-hectare plot with the thatched 800-square-metre family home he had built.

He moved into well-known international referee Tappe Henning's house. There were three of them living there: Tappe, a chap called François du Toit, and Joost – all divorced. Cynically, they called their new home the 'Divo (short for divorce) House'.

But Joost, instead of pursuing his old bachelor ways, found himself courting the lovely Amor. Finally he was legally free to try to capture the beautiful daughter of Italian immigrant Dario and *boeremeisie* Delyse Vittone. Although their relationship (despite what the press claimed) had been purely platonic up until his divorce, Joost found himself becoming increasingly attracted to Amor.

To his huge delight, she invited him to join her for dinner on Valentine's Day. Clad in their glad rags and with Joost at the wheel of Amor's BMW 330 convertible with the personalised registration, they descended on Vilamoura restaurant in the Sandton Sun hotel for their first 'official' date.

When Joost saw how she had arranged a secluded alcove for them and that only on their table were roses strewn among the cutlery, he realised that she had gone to a lot of trouble. So he decided he would make a special effort to be the perfect dining companion. When Amor began by ordering oysters, Joost ordered some too, despite never having eaten them before. As the evening progressed, they had more and more fun.

Driving home, Joost was as happy as the proverbial Larry. This dating game was such a pleasure, he idly mused, looking at the lovely girl sitting next to him. At that exact moment the lovely girl interrupted his reveries by writhing restlessly in her seat; suddenly his date, the luscious Amor, had a pained expression on her face and both hands firmly clutched to her stomach. 'What's the matter?' inquired her gallant chauffeur.

'I'm not sure – but something is terribly wrong. You can't believe the stomach pains I'm experiencing.'

Joost was about to suggest that they go to an emergency pharmacy or a doctor when Amor suddenly yelled at him, 'Oh my God! Please stop the car – hurry!'

Joost pulled over and braked at the same time. Before he could do anything, Amor had released her seatbelt, opened the door, jumped out and, pulling down her panties, squatted next to the vehicle. In that excruciatingly embarrassing moment – courtesy of a bad oyster – the universe dropped out of Amor's bottom.

Despite what was appearing in the press, Amor says she never had anything to do with Joost's divorce. 'Getting divorced is a long process, and Joost was literally weeks away from his when we met. So logically I couldn't have had anything to do with it. Besides that, I wasn't looking for anyone when I met him. I had just come out of a relationship and was sick of men. They all just wanted one thing,' she laughs.

Tertius Pickard

1995 World Cup: the Springboks sing the national anthem before their match against Western Samoa

Duif du Toit

Joost is pursued by New Zealand's Frank Bunce, 1996

Joost and Ruben Kruger lift the Currie Cup after the Blue Bulls' victory in 1998

With André Venter, who was rated as one of the fittest rugby players of his time, but is sadly now paralysed

Joost and Justin Marshall, his toughest opponent

Tertius Pickard

Australia's George Gregan and former compatriot Tiaan Strauss try to bring Joost down

Duif du Toit

Carlos Spencer and Tana Umaga can only look on as Joost scores against the All Blacks
in the 1999 Tri-Nations

Joost scores in the corner against England at the 1999 World Cup

Passing the ball in the 2002 Currie Cup final,
which the Bulls won

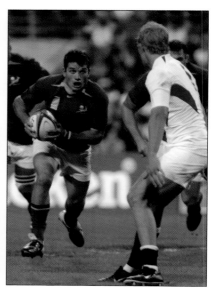

Joost makes a typical attacking run at
England during the 2003 World Cup

Joost and Amor's wedding day, December 2002. On the left are
Gustav and Mariana van der Westhuizen, and on the right are Delyse and Dario Vittone

On honeymoon in Mauritius, December 2002: Joost's lounger collapses

Three South African sporting heroes:
David Frost, Joost and Ernie Els at the 1999 British Open, St Andrews

With Mike Tyson and Brian Mitchell in 2008

Teaching Jordan how to hold a rugby ball, on his first visit to Loftus

Kylie: her favourite place

With Jordan and Kylie making houses on the beach

Joost and David Gemmell at work on *Joost: The Man in the Mirror*

Ducks doing morning lengths at the Shack

Joost reading about himself – can't put it down

'Mind you, we got on very well. We seemed to click on another level to what I had experienced with other men I dated.'

Amor mentions that Joost's ex-wife Marlene had appeared on the TV programme *Carte Blanche* almost a year before Amor met Joost. When Marlene was asked whether she would have married a rugby player if she had her life over again, she said no.

'I remember my dad once overhearing me talking to Joost on the phone and saying to me, with a bit of an Italian snarl, "He's married." But after my dad met him, it didn't take long before they got on. Joost won him over. One evening my dad walked into my room and sat down on my bed. I got all nervous, as one does, because I knew he wanted to talk. Then he cleared his throat. "Oh dear …" I thought.' She laughs. 'Anyway, all he said was, "You're going to marry that guy. Just be careful." It was weird.

'I had to teach Joost not to be so abrupt on the phone,' Amor laughs. 'We would be talking and suddenly he'd say he had to go. He would just say goodbye and put the phone down. One day I called him back and said that in future he was to wait for me to finish before he just said goodbye. From then on he would end every conversation by saying, "*Is jy nou klaar gepraat?*"

'As for the Valentine's Day dinner, we were in my car because Joost had arrived at my house on his motorbike. It was a wonderful evening, albeit with a bit of a disastrous end. But the interesting thing was that we both found the incident so funny. I remember looking at Joost and he had his head on his arms, which were folded on the steering wheel, and he was just killing himself laughing.

'At one stage he said, "And you've got your name on your number plate, *Amor GP*, so everyone knows who you are as they go past. I can just hear them saying …" he was almost hysterical by now,' she says, laughing, '"… check Amor's bought a piece of land and is marking her territory." So something that could have sunk some relationships just made us feel more comfortable with each other.'

Two months later, on 28 April 2002, the couple got engaged. That same year, on 21 December, they were married in a formal wedding attended by 150 guests at Aviente in Muldersdrif. Both sets of parents seemed comfortable with the union. Joost's folks had liked Marlene, but in reality very rarely saw her because Joost had visited them only infrequently.

Ever since he took up with Amor, they found that Joost came round more often, and so they saw much more of Amor than they ever did of Marlene.

Life for the two media sweethearts was very public. They were constantly on the covers of all sorts of publications.

When asked if they had ever 'sold' themselves to be on a cover, Joost says, 'Everybody thinks we have, but this is how it worked. Firstly, we never approached any magazine and said, "We're getting married – pay us for being on your cover." *They* approached *us* and asked for the rights to our wedding, in turn offering to pick up the cost of our honeymoon. So of course we accepted the deal.' (They spent their honeymoon in the Carribean and at Disneyland in Florida – fully funded by *Huisgenoot* magazine in return for exclusive rights to publish photographs from the honeymoon.)

'The only time we were actually paid money was for the rights to the births of our children. We did negotiate fees for the stories about Kylie and Jordan when they were born. But that money went straight into accounts in the kids' names for their education.'

Apart from that, Joost insists that they have never received anything for their appearances in magazines or on covers.

Joost says: 'The perception is, "They must have been paid because they are on the cover and are thus making money out of the magazine's sales. We therefore have the right to pry into their lives."'

During 2003, Joost arrived home from training and Amor presented him with a piece of paper. 'You are going to become a daddy,' she said. When Joost finally worked it out, he realised the paper contained the results of a pregnancy test.

'I dropped my boots and grabbed Amor. I had tears running down my face.'

The couple decided to be mature about the situation and tell their parents only after the first 12 weeks of pregnancy, which are supposedly quite risky. Half an hour later Joost was on the phone to his mother: 'Ma, Ma, Ma! Amor is pregnant!'

When Jordan was born, the Van der Westhuizens hadn't yet decided on a name for him, partly because they were waiting to see if Amor was having a boy or a girl. When it comes to naming children, the Afrikaans tradition holds that the husband will name the first son after his father; the second son will be named after the husband's mother's father, and a third son will be named after the husband. The same happens with girls, using the female side.

Joost and Amor decided they were going to break with tradition, although, having made the decision, they then took almost six months to settle on a name. Eventually Joost decided it had to be 'Jordan' after his sporting idol, the black American basketball player Michael Jordan.

'The amazing thing is,' says Joost, 'that Jordan *loves* basketball. His favourite TV show is *High School Musical*, and he always wants me to shoot hoops with him.'

When their daughter was born it was Amor's turn, and she chose the name Kylie, after her music hero Kylie Minogue. It hasn't been established yet whether Kylie is going to want to sing with her mother, but Amor says that she won't be surprised if it happens.

19

Rudolf Straeuli

The two things Joost remembers most about Rudolf Straeuli's reign as Springbok coach are Kamp Staaldraad (Camp Barbed Wire) and his own retirement from rugby.

Straeuli was the first of Joost's coaches with whom he had actually once played. Initially he thought their previous association as players might impact the new order, but there were never any problems. Later Joost felt it might even have worked in his favour: 'Having played with me, Rudolf knew exactly what I could deliver. Unfortunately there was also a negative aspect to this, as having played for the Springboks himself, he knew all the little tricks and scams the players got up to. He always knew where the fire-escape doors were,' laughs Joost. 'It was a classic case of poacher turned gamekeeper.'

However, some of the players found Straeuli's 'spying' on them unsettling.

Kamp Staaldraad was widely condemned in the press as an indication of the absurd levels to which Springbok rugby had sunk, and was later blamed for the poor showing of the team in the 2003 World Cup. But Joost still thinks it was a good experience, the purpose of which, according to him, was misunderstood by everyone.

'Before Kamp Staaldraad, Rudolf took the four senior players – Bobby Skinstad, Corné Krige, John Smit and me – away for the weekend to a farm north of Vaalwater. It was an unbelievable place, something like 20 000 hectares, with a fantastic lodge – apparently it belonged to [controversial businessman] Douw Steyn. When we got there, we were introduced to then president

Year	Vs	Score	Scrumhalf	Flyhalf	Captain	Tries
2002		SA-Other				
	Wales	34-19	Bolla Conradie	André Pretorius	Bobby Skinstad	
	Wales	19-8	Bolla Conradie	André Pretorius	Bobby Skinstad	
	Argentina	49-29	Craig Davidson	André Pretorius	Corné Krige	
	Samoa	60-18	Bolla Conradie	André Pretorius	Corné Krige	
	New Zealand	20-41	Bolla Conradie	André Pretorius	Corné Krige	
	Australia	27-38	Bolla Conradie	André Pretorius	Corné Krige	
	New Zealand	23-30	Neil de Kock	André Pretorius	Corné Krige	
	Australia	33-31	Neil de Kock	André Pretorius	Corné Krige	
	France	10-30	Neil de Kock	André Pretorius	Corné Krige	
	Scotland	6-21	Bolla Conradie	Butch James	Corné Krige	
	England	3-53	Bolla Conradie	André Pretorius	Corné Krige	
2003						
	Scotland	29-25	Joost	Louis Koen	Joost	
	Scotland	28-19	Joost	Louis Koen	Joost	
	Argentina	26-25	Craig Davidson	Louis Koen	Corné Krige	
	Australia	26-22	Joost	Louis Koen	Corné Krige	
	New Zealand	16-52	Joost	Louis Koen	Corné Krige	
	Australia	9-29	Craig Davidson	Louis Koen	Corné Krige	

Year	Vs	Score	Scrumhalf	Flyhalf	Captain	Tries
2003						
	New Zealand	11-19	Joost	Louis Koen	Corné Krige	
	Uruguay	72-6	Joost	Louis Koen	Joost	3
	England	6-25	Joost	Louis Koen	Corné Krige	
	Georgia	46-19	Neil de Kock	Derick Hougaard	John Smit	
	Samoa	60-10	Joost	Derick Hougaard	Corné Krige	
	New Zealand	9-29	Joost	Derick Hougaard	Corné Krige	
Tests: won 12, lost 11						

Nelson Mandela. He sat and chatted with us and generally just wished us well. He said he knew we would make the country proud. He also gave us all letters signed by him, thanking us.'

23 May 2003

Dear Joost

Although I keep a lower profile these days, I still like to take a keen interest in the Springboks. I know today is one of the most important days in your preparation for this year's World Cup. Today is the day that six individuals will begin to be forged into a unique leadership team.

Six people who will be stronger than the sum of their parts. Six people who will stand together in the good times and the bad, who will take a little less than their share of the credit, and a little more of the blame.

I want you all to be proud to be in such a privileged position, yet humble to have the honour of being our nation's finest rugby players. I always remember the axiom: a leader ... is like a shepherd. He stays behind the flock, letting the most nimble go out ahead, whereupon the others follow, not realising that all along they are being directed from behind.

The World Cup is a rare event held only a handful of times, and as you know few men can claim to have been part of victorious teams. There have been many special moments, but personally I will never forget that thrilling day in June 1995 when our fledgling nation celebrated the Springboks winning the World Cup at the first attempt. South Africa was truly united in a way never seen before.

Joost, I will never forget the pass you threw for the winning drop in 1995. It was close in 1999, but now you have the opportunity to rekindle that winning feeling. You are the most experienced player in the squad, and are going to your third World Cup. I want you to use all your knowledge and experience wisely to guide and build belief in the younger players.

I believe that together this leadership team, through dedication and application, can bring the Webb Ellis Trophy home in November. All the best as you strive to join the elite group of past winners. Do not forget, you have the support of a nation behind you.

Best regards

NR Mandela

Much later, on 30 August 2003 in Pretoria, just after the Springbok squad had been announced, the players were told to get into their shorts, training jerseys, socks and walking shoes and to meet downstairs. 'There was a funny moment when Joe van Niekerk's girlfriend arrived to give him some face cream – he was told to leave it in his room because he wouldn't be needing it where he was going,' laughs Joost.

When asked what the players thought was going on, Joost replies, 'Everyone was in high spirits. I think they thought we were going on a sort of high-school camp.'

From having to drag three different-size tractor tyres that were chained together to standing naked in freezing water for hours; from having to spend the night in a dark hole in the ground to leopard-crawling across ploughed fields in T-shirts and shorts, Kamp Staaldraad was certainly unlike any school camp and not for the faint-hearted.

In a newspaper interview in *The Weekender* on 21 March 2009, Joost reprised his pet complaint:

DG: **You supported Kamp Staaldraad at the time. It was subsequently universally condemned. How did that affect your views on it?**

JvdW: I hate lies. The media reported it wrongly. It was the best time of my life – it made me tough, and I think that's why I'm coping now with all this other nonsense. It was total mind fitness. I came out a stronger person. A lot of guys couldn't cope with it and used the media as a comfort zone to explain their failure. When we left Kamp Staaldraad, we were ONE team. We could have won anything. But before we could cement that oneness, we stopped at Warmbaths and the guys saw the dishonest stuff that had been written by Mark Keohane. He contacted people individually to support his rubbish. Then the team split. Remember that before it started, SARU signed it off. Every single thing about that camp, they signed off. Where are those documents?

DG: **You don't like Keohane?**

JvdW: The darkest day in South African rugby history was when Mark Keohane was appointed media liaison for the Springboks. Every single confidential meeting we had as a team was in the press the next morning. The guys then started to doubt each other. And then, when the *Argus* bought the tape from a guy who three weeks later killed himself, it showed me how rotten things were. Video operator Dale McDermott was on Kamp Staaldraad and he sold the tape for about thirty grand. He then later shot himself.

Kamp Staaldraad was run by Adriaan Heijns, a former South African Police Task Force commander who had his own security company. Ramboesque and forceful, he soon took charge of the unsuspecting aspirant World Cup rugby players. As the men steadily moved in ones and twos from the function where the 2003 World Cup squad had been announced onto the waiting bus under the gaze of Heijns and his gun-toting assistants, they were all slightly nervous but generally unconcerned. They were in the World Cup squad, they were Springboks, they were fit and strong – how bad could the camp be?

As it turned out, a lot worse than they could ever have imagined.

After a couple of hours' travel, the luxury bus stopped without warning on a dirt road in the middle of nowhere. Heijns instructed the players to step off and strip naked.

'When you are in the nude in a change room it feels natural because it is such a regular occurrence,' says Joost. 'But when you are standing naked in the middle of nowhere, you definitely feel embarrassed and shy. You have a weird feeling that you're doing something wrong.'

Just two or three hours earlier they had all been strutting around smartly dressed at a function with other equally smartly attired guests – now, suddenly, they were standing naked in the bush, a long way from that glamorous gathering.

Their clothes were then searched by Heijns and his armed henchmen (no doubt they had been tipped off about Joe van

Niekerk's face cream). The players were given red rugby jerseys and told that from then on they would be known only as numbers and not by their names. Joost was No. 55.

Dressed in their new gear, the increasingly disconcerted players were summarily loaded onto a truck, which then fitfully lumbered off into the dark, foreboding bush. When their new mode of bumpy transport finally ground to a halt in what they could barely identify in the darkness as a clearing, the players reluctantly and very dispiritedly vacated the vehicle.

They were immediately divided into pairs by what the increasingly unhappy group had decided were 'guards', not helpers or assistants. Each pair was then given a huge log to carry. According to 'No. 55', the logs were of such a massive size and so thick in diameter that they were almost impossible to lift, never mind carry.

After just minutes of carrying the logs, the players found them so heavy that they had to shift them from shoulder to shoulder. If any pair dropped their log while making the increasingly precarious and difficult swap from one side to the other, the entire group had to go back to the starting point.

The logs were only the beginning. Once they had completed playing lumberjacks, the players were divided into teams of 10. Each team was then ordered to carry a set of three tractor tyres, joined together with heavy metal chains, to a point in the far distance. Because the tyres were different sizes, they were extremely difficult to hold onto.

'It seemed to take a bloody eternity,' says Joost, 'to move the tyres to where they had to go, and the whole time the guys were asking what relevance the exercise had. Everyone was very grumpy.' Having dumped the tyres at the designated spot, the reformed squad was made to alternately march and jog for what seemed like hours.

It was difficult to estimate how long each exercise took, says Joost, because when the players had been ordered to strip naked, the armed guards had taken their watches. To compound the group's discomfort, every time a player made a mistake, the whole squad was punished by being made to leopard-crawl through the burnt scrub or by having to do push-ups.

The mindless, incomprehensible series of exercises went on throughout the night. In the early hours of the morning, the exhausted players were finally allowed to rest, albeit briefly. By then a mind-numbing shock had permeated their weary bodies and the general mood of the group was one of extreme sullenness.

Next on the list of useful activities in Heijns's cutting-edge preparation of the squad for the 2003 World Cup? While standing naked in a freezing lake, each player had to pump up a rugby ball. The problem was that there were only three pumps. It therefore took an interminably long time for each player to get his ball pumped to the right pressure, which meant an equally interminably long time in the icy water.

At this stage, a mini revolt occurred when No. 44, Springbok captain Corné Krige, walked out of the lake. All but one of the players followed him. No. 22, prop forward Faan Rautenbach, stayed on in the ice-cold water. According to No. 44, the burly prop had sufficient body fat to survive longer than the rest of the guys. No. 22 might also have guessed that the boys would be back. He was right.

On realising what was going on, Heijns and his cronies, who were drinking beer and braaiing a few yards from the edge of the water, went ballistic and started shouting at the players to get back in the lake. Incensed at having their lunch so rudely disturbed, Heijns and the guards proceeded to fire live ammunition into the water on either side of the bedraggled, frozen group – who, surprise, surprise, swiftly returned to rejoin the freezing prop forward.

It is probably fortunate that the guards had live rounds in their guns. Who knows how the naked, frozen, disgruntled rugby players would have reacted had their guardians only fired blanks?

In his book *The Right Place at the Wrong Time*, No. 44 says it is one of his big regrets that he didn't keep on walking. 'Today I know what I should have done. I should have kept on walking out of the water, leading those players who wanted to follow their captain.'

Given No. 55's opinion that Kamp Staaldraad had been a good thing, it is not surprising that No. 44 continues: 'I should have walked right out of that lunatic asylum of a camp. But I knew that I would have needed the support of the senior players. I believe most of them would have backed me, but I was worried about Joost. He enjoyed that sort of stuff and had gone through it before – or something like it. And before the camp started he'd mentioned that those of us who didn't complete it might be thrown out of the squad. I therefore doubted he would have supported me.'

The madness continued. Next they had to fight each other because, according to Heijns, they didn't have proper respect for each other's abilities. They were given boxing gloves and headgear and told to fight pre-selected opponents.

No. 55 had to fight No. 70, Ashwin Willemse. Joost took no pleasure in smacking someone he really liked, he says, and sub-sequent events – at one stage No. 70 would accuse Joost of racist behaviour – demonstrated that the boxing definitely had a harm-ful effect on their relationship.

After another route march to nowhere, the harassed players had to run an obstacle course. Three small tins of lamb stew were the prize for the first team home. As it transpired, the team that ultimately completed the course in the fastest time generously shared the meagre rations with the other ravenous teams so that everyone at least got a small mouthful. By then the players were utterly famished, as they hadn't eaten anything since they left Pretoria 36 hours earlier.

In the next exercise, they were given a chicken leg, an egg and a match. The purpose of the task was to use the solitary match to start a fire with which to cook the leg and the egg. The group was split up, with players positioned far away from each other. They were not surprised by that stage – or impressed, for that matter – when they were instructed to eat neither egg nor chicken leg once these were cooked.

Some of the players had a lot of difficulty playing Boy Scouts, especially the city boys. However, they were explicitly prohibited from seeking help from each other. After having spent a couple of hours in the sub-zero lake, having to light and make a fire with precisely one match presented an interesting and, for some, considerable challenge. Joost doesn't know who did not manage to make a fire, but according to him there were definitely a few who didn't succeed.

Bizarrely, Joost says that lying next to a roaring fire under the stars alone in the bush was like being in a hotel room … 'It was awesome,' he says, without a hint of irony. 'I had time on my own. I thought about a lot of things, and it was so peaceful lying next to my own warm fire. In fact, I made one on either side of me – it was just magical.' He omits to mention that he was filthy, underdressed, starving and lying on burnt-out scrub in the middle of absolutely nowhere. The mind boggles.

The next morning, the guards checked if the food had been properly cooked. They carefully studied the chicken legs and then smashed the eggs on the wretched players' heads. If the eggs weren't sufficiently cooked, the yolk ran down the players' necks and faces, which, No. 55 says, most of them found degrading.

The litany of useful challenges the players had to complete continued with a raft-race across a dam. But first they had to build the rafts. They were divided into teams, and each team was given a couple of empty oil drums, some planks and a number of lengths of rope. After carefully constructing vessels they hoped wouldn't emulate the *Titanic*, they were no doubt thrilled when the ever-present guards instructed them to use a raft other than the one their team had constructed.

Despite the warped circumstances, the winning team, in a remarkable act of selflessness – presumably prompted by the earlier sharing of the tins of lamb stew – shared the spoils with the others. This time the prize was four small chocolate bars – the distribution didn't take long.

Joost mentions that the whole time they were on the camp, they were constantly given 'punishments' in the form of push-ups and being made to leopard-crawl across the fields for even the smallest 'transgressions'. How was it even possible to 'punish' them when the entire concept of the camp was, in essence, a monument to the god of punishment?

But wait – there's more. After the group had been forced to compete in a tug of war, three live chickens were produced as the prizes. Specific players were ordered to kill the unfortunate poultry. In a scene straight out of a horror movie, a player not well versed in the forgotten art of slaughtering livestock at rugby practice tried to beat one of the fowls to death by smashing the luckless bird on the ground. (In the end No. 55 had to lend a hand to help dispatch the poor fowl to the great coop in the sky.) The executioners then plucked and cooked their ill-fated victims. (Perhaps the architects of Kamp Staàldraad had thought that killing chickens might be a useful skill to acquire should South Africa come up against France in the World Cup?)

Despite the camp drawing to an end, Heijns and his merry men managed to squeeze in a last few Machiavellian schemes. One involved crawling naked through a pipe into a big pit covered by a tarpaulin. Just in case the players got too comfortable in the pitch-black darkness and forgot where they were, they were regularly hosed down with cold water to the accompaniment of the melodic strains of the New Zealand haka – the Kiwi battle call was repeatedly blasted at the players from a couple of large speakers placed near the pit.

Joost suddenly remembers that he had forgotten to mention the ammunition boxes filled with cement that the players had

had to carry up a hill and back while lugging a short piece of steel railway track with a ball and chain attached. He thinks for a while and says, 'That was just before we had to do the tug of war.' Curious how it is more important to No. 55 to recall the chronology of events than to comment on how awful carrying such an impossibly discordant combination of heavy, unbalanced items must have been.

The last 'big' exercise they had to complete was to jump out of a military helicopter into the freezing lake. Joost estimates that they were dropped from a height of about 20 metres above the water. After the jump they had to march back to the camp, where they found a huge tent that, in their shattered collective frame of mind, equated to incomparable luxury. They all crammed inside and collapsed into a fitful sleep. Joost mentions that at that point they all managed to fit into the tent, but later, when they had showered and got into clean clothes, they couldn't all get under their erstwhile canvas haven at the same time.

'The reason was,' he says, 'that when we were all scruffy and dirty and frozen, we didn't care how physically close we got to each other and whether we touched or lay on one another, as we were desperate to keep warm and snatch some sleep. But when we were all respectable again, it felt awkward to be too familiar.'

The team left a while later for the 2003 World Cup in Australia, and every time the Springboks played a match, something about Kamp Staaldraad leaked out in the press back home. It subsequently surfaced that the team video analyst, Dale McDermott, had filmed most of what had happened at Kamp Staaldraad and sold it to the *Argus* newspaper in Cape Town. (McDermott later committed suicide by shooting himself in the head – believed by many to be a direct consequence of being sacked by SARFU and feeling guilty for having sold the video footage to the press. He was a nice chap, reckons No. 55.)

After returning from the failed attempt to regain the Webb Ellis Trophy, Joost decided he wanted to have a breakfast with the sponsors and any other interested businesspeople to clear up some of the misconceptions about Kamp Staaldraad and the negativity with which it had been reported.

'Everybody made out that Kamp Staaldraad was 99 per cent negative,' he says. 'It wasn't. There were good times. We sang "Nkosi Sikelele" when we were so, so tired; we laughed and we bonded. I wanted to show the real side of what had happened.'

Joost phoned a number of the senior players. 'They all supported the idea – they all said they would back me, but the moment the press got wind of the breakfast, they backed down. I was furious.' In the end the support of those players added up to nothing ...

As an extension of the breakfast idea, Adriaan Heijns wanted to bring out a DVD showing exactly what had happened at the camp with none other than its greatest fan, No. 55, as presenter. But Joost couldn't accept the job, as he was now part of Super-Sport.

'A number of people accused me of promoting that video,' says Joost. 'Johann Rupert even accused me of actually being part of the production of the video. But I never was.' An accusation, a video – a recurring theme in Joost van der Westhuizen's life, it would seem.

It is still debatable whether Kamp Staaldraad had any benefit for the Springboks' rugby. In his book *The Right Place at the Wrong Time*, former Springbok captain Corné Krige says:

And, in hindsight, I am convinced that [Kamp Staaldraad] was of no value whatsoever. What we went through was a complete waste of time. In our quest to win the Rugby World Cup, it didn't make any difference at all. Indeed after the tournament, some people used the camp as an excuse for why we lost the World Cup. I never agreed with that, but I certainly did not agree with the concept of the camp as part of our preparation either. Not at all.

In all likelihood, Joost's background was at least partly responsible for him finding the exercise uplifting and 'character-building' and why, in a perverse way, he actually enjoyed it. As a nation, Afrikaners have always been used to hardship and deprivation. They fought the elements, they tamed the land and they were not strangers to conflict. They were physical people. They would rather do something than philosophise about it.

It was the nature of the beast. People who depart their home-lands for far-distant shores to search for a better life are not soft or acquiescent. Hardship and adversity were, to them, simply the price you paid for what you wanted. And in their struggle against nature and other nations – like the Zulus and the English – they bonded with and relied on each other. They forged unbreakable friendships in the heat of battle, in the midst of privation. Their relationships weren't founded on good times. Nothing came easily and, if it did, it wasn't worth anything to them.

20

Lunch

In 2003, on the way home from training for the World Cup, Joost's cellphone rang. He presumed it was Amor, phoning to find out when he would be home, but he couldn't see the caller's identity, so in his inimitable way he barked, 'Joost?'

'Hello, Joost, this is Nelson Mandela,' said a voice suspiciously similar to the former president's.

'Ja?' said Joost, a bit thrown.

'Joost, I would like to invite you and your wife for lunch.' Astonishingly, to Joost it sounded *exactly* like Mandela – but obviously, he thought, it couldn't be!

'When?' asked a by-then disbelieving Joost.

'Would Thursday in two weeks' time at my residence in Houghton suit you?'

'Whatever,' said Joost, having decided that it was probably well-known radio and TV personality Darren Scott trying to trick him. Smiling and with ever-so-slight insolence he added, 'I'm on my way home and I'll ask Amor if we're available. Call me in half an hour.'

'Thank you very much. I will call you later.'

'He really does the old man's voice bloody well,' Joost thought.

When he got home, he walked into the bedroom, dropped his boots in the corner and said to Amor, 'You'll never believe it. Darren has been pretending he's Mandela. He thinks he is going to catch me out—' and with that his phone rang.

'Hello, this is Mandela again.'

'Ja,' said Joost, smiling at Amor. Pointing to the phone, he exaggeratedly mouthed, 'Darren.'

'If you and your lovely wife are coming for lunch, what would you like to eat?'

Joost said, 'Hold on.' He turned to Amor and asked loudly, 'What do we want to eat at Mr Mandela's house, my love?'

Laughing and playing along, Amor replied, 'What about chicken? Yes, let's have chicken and rice. That would be great.'

'Chicken and rice would be good,' Joost said to 'Mr Mandela'.

'And I believe your wife is Italian? Would she like any particular wine?'

'You talk to her,' said Joost, trying to suppress a laugh and handing the phone to Amor.

'Hello, Mr Mandela,' Amor said. 'I love red wine – any type and *copius* amounts will do.'

Joost took the phone back and agreed they would see 'Mr Mandela' in two weeks' time. Joost and Amor laughed and thought no more of it.

Two weeks later, on the Wednesday, Zelda la Grange from Mr Mandela's office called to confirm the next day's lunch. 'Oh my God, that was Zelda! It really was him!' said Joost to a horrified Amor.

The next day they arrived at the lunch still squirming inwardly. Joost had met Mr Mandela before (at the farm before Kamp Staaldraad), which made it ever so slightly easier for him, but Amor hadn't and was very nervous.

After the normal small talk about the weather, Joost couldn't contain himself any longer and apologised for the disrespect he and Amor had shown when Mr Mandela had called to invite them for lunch. Feeling extraordinarily pathetic, a blushing Joost lamely explained how he had thought someone was playing a prank on him and Amor. Amor just sat there, mortified.

Mr Mandela threw back his head and laughed delightedly. 'Please don't be concerned,' he said. 'It's happened before. You certainly aren't the first. Nor, I am quite sure, will you be the last.'

At which juncture Amor felt that she, too, should apologise.

Mr Mandela stopped her. 'It was very funny on my side, because I could hear you weren't convinced it was me,' he said, smiling. 'In any event, I still arranged *copius* amounts of red wine for you.' Amor blushed.

At lunch, Mandela seated them. 'Amor, you sit here in Graça's place, and Joost, you sit here on this side, next to me.'

During lunch, and by now feeling far more comfortable, Joost politely asked Madiba why he had invited them over. The former president replied that he often had lunches with well-known South Africans.

From that point on, Amor relaxed, and when an errant grain of rice attached itself to Madiba's bottom lip, she simply reached over and brushed it off as one would with a messy child. Madiba just laughed and said, 'I must be getting old – Oprah also did that to me.'

On the way out, as they were all standing on the front porch saying their goodbyes, Joost plucked up the courage and said, 'Excuse me, sir, but would you mind terribly if we had our picture taken with you?'

Mandela beamed at him and replied, 'You know, Joost, when we got to this front door and you were about to leave, I thought I'd done something very wrong, because you were the first people ever who didn't want a picture. I am hugely relieved,' he smiled. 'It would be an honour.'

21

Rugby World Cup 2003

In 2003, for the fifth year in a row, South Africa finished last in the Tri-Nations competition. The Springboks beat Australia 26-22 in Cape Town, but lost badly to New Zealand in Pretoria (16-52). The return match against Australia in Brisbane was lost 9-29, and New Zealand beat the luckless Boks 19-11 in Dunedin. (A match that South Africans will only remember for a fantastic try by prop Richard Bands.)

But even before the start of the Tri-Nations, the Springboks had been struggling. None of their performances were confident or assured. In the first two tests of the year, they unconvincingly and narrowly scraped past Scotland 29-25 in Durban, then won 28-19 in Johannesburg. They came within a last-minute penalty by flyhalf Louis Koen of losing to Argentina in Port Elizabeth, just scraping home 26-25.

Rudolf Straeuli kept changing his team, which never gave combinations time to settle down and learn how to play with each other. One of Straeuli's major concerns was that the players would become complacent about their place in the team, but his continuous changes had an adverse effect on the players' confidence. 'They were too scared to do anything,' says Joost, 'because if they cocked up, they knew they would be out of the team. You definitely play better if you are not continually worrying about whether you will be playing next week's match.'

In the aftermath of Kamp Staaldraad, far from having the 'bonded', loyal and committed players Straeuli had thought would emerge from the bush excursion, he found himself with an

unstructured, nervous bunch of Springboks who not only doubted their ability to win matches, but also distrusted their coach.

As a former Springbok, Straeuli knew all the scams and tricks
the players could get up to. Instead of letting them be, as had
always been the way, he used his players' knowledge to try to catch
them out and clamp down on their fun. His attitude engendered
distrust in the players.

'They also felt that Rudolf wanted to control everything,' says
Joost.

Mark Keohane, communications manager for the Springboks,
writing in the English press, said, 'He [Straeuli] asked me what my
greatest criticism of him was. I said his paranoia, the clandestine
manner in which the team was being run, the listening to people
who further fuel his paranoia, the lack of communication, the
mind-games played with individuals, the constant changing of
things, the instability in his decision-making and his being too
aware of pleasing every provincial and racial faction before making
a decision.' (Keohane had resigned in protest at what he described
as 'ongoing prejudice in South African rugby'.)

The article was Keohane's response to an incident involving
Bulls lock Geo Cronjé, who had refused to share a room with a
coloured player, Quinton Davids. The story made headlines world-
wide. It seemed as if years after it had been abolished, apartheid
had raised its ugly head at a Springbok training camp under the
control of Rudolf Straeuli. SARFU conducted an inquiry, but in
the end came to the baffling conclusion that they could find no
proof of racial misconduct on Cronjé's part.

In the end, to put an end to the controversy, both players
were asked to leave the World Cup squad – a decision that was
generally considered extremely harsh on Davids.

In *The Right Place at the Wrong Time*, Corné Krige writes, 'In
Quinton's case, the decision to exclude him from the World Cup
was totally unacceptable. After all, what had he done wrong?'

The Springbok captain goes on to say, 'Quinton is a good man and he deserved to go to Australia. His situation was handled very badly, and he was very upset about missing the World Cup ... Quinton deserved to be in the squad.'

Starting their 2003 World Cup campaign in Perth, Australia, South Africa found themselves in Pool C with Uruguay, Georgia, Samoa and England. Beating the Poms would put the Springboks on the high road, where they would in all likelihood come up against Wales in the quarter-finals. Losing to England would condemn them to facing the mighty All Blacks instead.

In the first match against Uruguay, scrumhalf and stand-in captain Joost van der Westhuizen scored three tries to earn him the South African try-scoring record of 38 test tries. As it turned out, it would be the last time he scored in the green-and-gold jersey of the Springboks. South Africa won the game 72-6. (These were the only tries Van der Westhuizen scored in his nine starts under Straeuli.)

Speaking in the *Springbok Saga* video series, Corné Krige says there had been too much focus on beating England in Perth. 'I always felt that Rudi was building up the England game to such an extent that, if we lost it, the players would feel our World Cup was over.'

Straeuli put England players' names on the tackle bags in what was probably an extension of the Kamp Staaldraad School of Mental Conditioning.

Psychologically, the Springboks were probably more mindful of the fact that they hadn't beaten England in the two teams' last four outings. Even worse, in the last game of 2002, England had thrashed South Africa 53-3. The more senior players may also have recalled that England had stopped Nick Mallett's test-winning run when it equalled New Zealand's record of 17 consecutive wins (England 27-South Africa 22).

To further exacerbate the less-than-ideal preparation for the match, a horrible off-the-field incident occurred when Louis Koen's pregnant wife Lelani was held up at gunpoint in Johannesburg and her handbag was stolen. Although it is debatable whether the incident directly affected the young flyhalf's game, as he was his normal accurate self when it came to place-kicking. Apart from one of his drop kicks being charged down (regrettably ending up in a try for England), he never made any obvious errors.

England won the game 25-6 courtesy of a perfect kicking display by flyhalf Jonny Wilkinson.

The Springboks then travelled to Sydney to take on Georgia. As expected, the Boks won this game (46-19), but not without a bit of resistance from the never-say-die Georgians.

The match is probably best remembered for the debuts of John Smit as captain (he was later to captain the victorious Springboks in the 2007 World Cup, and is currently the most capped international captain, having captained the Springboks 60 times) and Schalk Burger on the side of the scrum. Schalk managed to score a try on debut, much to the delight of his proud father, Schalk Burger Sr, who had represented the Springboks from 1984 to 1986 and who had travelled over for the game.

Then it was off to Brisbane to play Samoa. The game had hardly kicked off when Joost van der Westhuizen put away Joe van Niekerk for a try. The Springboks were overwhelming favourites to win the match and coasted home 60-10.

But the World Cup only began in earnest for the South Africans as they headed for Melbourne to take on New Zealand. Strangely, despite the Springboks' pretty abysmal year, reports from inside the Kiwi camp revealed that they were very nervous about the quarter-final match. After their semi-final loss to France in the 1999 World Cup, there was such a lot of pressure from their supporters back home that they didn't dare stumble again.

At the beginning of the World Cup, Joost van der Westhuizen had announced that he would be retiring after the final. Despite the unpromising start to the year, the no-surrender veteran of 88 tests (he ended on 89) still believed in his heart that, come the end of the tournament, the Springboks would be contesting the final.

It was not to be. The Kiwis took the game by the scruff of the neck and never let the Springboks become a threat. In the end, they won fairly easily (29-9). New Zealand then repeated their 1999 performance by going out in the semi-final (10-22) to Australia.

In the 79th minute of the final, with England leading 14-11, South African referee André Watson awarded Australia a penalty. Elton Flatley, the Wallaby inside centre, converted the penalty with the last kick in normal playing time to tie the score 14-all and take the match into extra time (20 minutes) – the third World Cup final in succession to go beyond 80 minutes.

England opened the scoring in extra time with a Wilkinson penalty, but with two-and-a-half minutes of extra time remaining, Australia was awarded another penalty, which Flatley kicked successfully – score: 17-all. Then, with 21 seconds left before sudden death, in a scene reminiscent of the dying moments of the 1995 World Cup final, Jonny Wilkinson kicked a drop goal for England to defeat two-times world champions Australia 20-17.

As Joost walked off the field after losing the quarter-final game, knowing it was for the last time, something made him look back. As he did, he saw Corné Krige and John Smit clapping him off. 'It was just such a nice thing for them to do,' he says. As he took his place on the bench, he looked down and smiled. 'I suddenly realised it was all over.' Blue Bulls captain Adriaan Richter's words all those years ago flashed through his mind.

As Joost sat next to the field, many thoughts raced through his head. But as he summed up his career, he felt immensely privileged that he had succeeded in his goal of playing in three World Cups. The other achievements, he thought, would sink in later. But for that moment in time, sitting on the bench, he just felt extraordinarily satisfied.

'I probably could have carried on for another season,' he says, 'but I wanted to stop playing while I was still good enough to wear a Springbok jersey.'

22

A new life

In January of 2004, Joost's son Jordan was born. 'It was wonderful,' the proud father says, 'but I honestly don't think any relationship can ever be prepared for the changes that having a child brings. And can I ask you about one thing that still mystifies me? Why do babies get bloody wind? I nearly went *mal* trying to get Jordan to burp.'

Joost recounts how, in the early hours of the morning, Amor had handed Jordan to him so that he could have a go at burping him. When Amor later came to check how he was doing, she found Joost on his feet, fast asleep but still whacking the little mite on his back. She immediately woke up her somnolent spouse. 'Gently, gently,' she admonished him. 'You're just supposed to lightly pat him, not bloody wallop him!'

'I became an expert at burping Jordan when I started handling him like a rugby ball,' Joost smiles. 'I would hold him face down in the palm of my hand and then put my other hand on him quickly, as though I was going to pass him, and he would just suddenly burp. As small as Jordan was, he probably thought, "If I don't burp, I might get flung somewhere ..."' Joost laughs at his own joke.

Another occasion he remembers fondly is driving home with the newborn Jordan. 'I couldn't believe it, but I was so concerned about Amor and Jordan that I found I couldn't drive faster than 40 kilometres an hour – all the way home!'

But not everything was all sweetness and light. Apart from performing menial childminding functions like changing nappies, Joost wasn't really needed much. 'Also, when they are that young,' he adds, 'they aren't exactly a bundle of fun. I mean, apart from changing nappies and feeding Jordan, there wasn't much for me to do. And Amor and I couldn't just go out and do things together, like we can now. I suppose that's why, at that time, I was finding it difficult to stop being a rugger bugger.'

At the beginning of 2004, Joost received a call from Gert Roets of SuperSport. They wanted to give the retired Springbok a trial on a programme called *Super Rugby*, with co-presenters Naas Botha (former Springbok flyhalf) and Kobus Wiese (former Springbok lock). 'Apart from doing the actual programme, *Super Rugby*,' Joost says, 'I also started doing match commentaries. I thoroughly enjoyed the experience. It was fascinating to be on the other side of the microphone for a change. But I had to learn quickly.'

He laughs. 'In the beginning of 2005, SuperSport had their huge annual planning meeting, during which they discussed the way forward. They discussed how the presenters would be dressed, their guidelines for the year, areas in which they could improve – the sort of stuff that would normally be covered at a planning session.'

All the presenters, English and Afrikaans, from around the country attended the meeting.

Says Joost, still laughing, 'The big boss, Imtiaz Patel [the CEO of SuperSport], stood up and opened his speech by saying, "Welcome, I'm glad you are all here. As you know, the reason we are meeting is simply so that we can all improve in what we do. I mean, look at Joost here," and Imtiaz pointed at me. "In his first year he was a DISASTER as a commentator – but look at him now. Look how he has improved." Everyone cracked up.'

Smiling and shaking his head, Joost said ironically, 'Thank you for telling me, Mr Patel, especially in front of everybody …' Joost honestly hadn't known he'd been so awful.

His biggest problem, Joost says, was that he didn't have a proper job description. So he created his own. 'My personal irritation was watching a game during which the commentator just told me what I was already seeing. I wanted more. So I decided my job would be to be an educator; I would try to explain to people what was behind the action they were seeing. I studied up on the rules and kept up with the changes in the laws.'

He also tried to make people understand *why* things happened on the field. For instance, what the player's thinking was behind a certain move or how tactics would change to accommodate different situations.

'I was also determined never, ever to criticise a player. I had had to endure so much criticism when I was playing, and it was infuriating. I wasn't going to fall into the same trap now. You can't believe how hard we trained and how we never intentionally stuffed up. But if you listen to some commentators, you would think we were deliberately trying to make mistakes.'

Joost reckons that Imtiaz Patel was correct. 'Not so much about me being a DISASTER,' he laughs, 'but about me improving. I learnt to say things in fewer words – to sum up quickly, but still give a proper explanation about what was happening in a partic- ular instance. I also learnt to stop using slang and to speak proper Afrikaans. For example, I stopped saying things like, "Hierdie is 'n *great game* …"'

Joost also learnt that 'silence can tell a story; a sound can tell a story – like after a fantastic try, all I would say was, "Wow!" instead of "and he runs down the wing and cuts in, and he dives over …" I mean, think about it – everyone is seeing the same try, so why tell them what they are seeing for themselves?'

Joost started his commentating career doing 'colour' commen- tary (commentaries on highlights or replays) with the doyen of South African commentators, Hugh Bladen. Both loved and hated for his enthusiastic and knowledgeable commentary style, Hugh is often better known for a terrible accident that happened in which he very nearly died.

Interview with Hugh Bladen

To move ahead to the time you fell over the balcony of a hotel in Durban and nearly killed yourself; what happened there?

We were down in Durban for the Toyota Championships and decided to stay in the Edward Hotel, so we didn't have too far to drive – I was going up the north coast to Sinkwazi the next day. Well, after the games we had a cocktail party, as one does at rugby; we then went to a private party at the Elangeni hotel, and later back to the Edward Hotel. My roommate, Ralph Hesketh-Maree, ordered toasted sandwiches as blotting paper before we went to bed, but I fell asleep before they came or I wasn't hungry. I don't remember anything, but I can only assume that during the early hours of the next morning, I must have had to relieve myself, was disoriented, went the wrong way and toppled over the outside balcony. I fell 25 metres onto a concrete ledge below.

What part of you hit the concrete first?

I landed on my feet. My ankles went through my heels. I was lucky – if I had landed on my head I would have been killed instantly. I also broke all my ribs and cracked my pelvis. The other thing is that it was the first of April, so when my roommate, Ralph, got a call from downstairs saying I was in an ambulance on the way to Addington Hospital, he thought it was an April fool's joke – until he saw I wasn't in my bed. I was in theatre for five hours and then two days after my admission to hospital, I developed acute renal failure; my lungs collapsed, so they put me on a ventilator; they removed my pancreas and they had to give me a tracheotomy – so talk about a mess. For the next twelve days, I was fighting for my life.

There was the odd light-hearted moment?

I suppose you can call it that. When the guy who discovered me on the balcony saw me, he said, 'How are you?' I was lying in a pool of blood, but apparently I looked up and said, 'I'm fine, thank you, and how are you?' He later phoned my brother Richard and asked if we had been strictly brought up. Also much later, I attended a Chris Burger memorial Fund dinner in a wheelchair. I was being pushed by Syd Nomis and I had takkies on with my dinner suit, when a youngster came up to me and said, 'I hope you realise by now that flyhalves can't fly.'

The Weekender, 8–9 November 2008

Hugh and Joost had a structure to their commentary: Bladen would commentate on the game while it was in progress, and Joost would talk through the replays. The nervous former Springbok quickly learnt how to time his comments to run the same length as the clip, because on a couple of occasions they would return to the game and Joost would find himself being cut off by Hugh mid-sentence.

'Initially I would feel quite stupid,' he says. 'I would be half-way through a technical explanation about something or other and Hugh would suddenly be calling what was happening at a line-out.'

When asked what it was like commentating with someone who used to commentate on *his* games, Joost replies, 'It was a great honour. But I soon realised Hugh had his own methods and, of course, his own style, and I knew I'd never be able to copy him. Also, I soon understood that I had to provide a different perspective on the game. Working with Hugh was a wonderful experience, and when I think about it, I was very lucky. I mean, right at the beginning of my commentating career I was learning from the best. Hugh is simply amazing.'

He adds: 'To be fair, I learnt something from all the guys I commentated with, like John van Rensburg – he was also fantastic. But Hugh just stands out.'

In 2009, when the video scandal broke, SuperSport suspended Joost from his commentating duties. He understands why, but just as Kitch Christie said when he was hired by the Bulls, 'You are hiring me for my brain, not for my body,' Joost feels Super-Sport hired him for his rugby knowledge and the fact that he was a well-known Springbok. He leaves unsaid that he wasn't hired for what went on in his private life.

'I understand that you can't completely divorce the private life of the commentators from their public persona,' he says, 'because ultimately they are the face of the SuperSport brand; but, interestingly, it doesn't seem to be much of a problem else-where.

'Shane Warne is one of the main commentators in the Ashes series currently taking place in England [the northern hemisphere summer of 2009]. I have nothing against him – I don't even know him – but he's certainly had an interesting private life. I think Shane is possibly the only other international sporting figure who has had more negative publicity than me.' He smiles wryly.

Although, when all is said and done, Joost is remarkably san-guine about his suspension. He still reckons SuperSport is one of the most professional companies he has ever had the pleasure of working for and candidly admits that he would like to work for them again.

He looks up and says, 'Off the record, do you think someone at SuperSport might read this book and give me another chance? I loved commentating, as I learnt a lot about the game and I thoroughly enjoyed being involved in rugby again.' He thinks for a minute, no doubt ruminating on the ending of this opus, shakes his head and says disconsolately, 'Nah, probably not.'

23

Writing Joost's book V

When I first met Joost and we discussed his suspension from commentating for SuperSport, I idly mentioned that I'd once written an article on sports commentators, published in Football Traveller *magazine. He asked for a copy to read. He really enjoyed the piece and suggested I send it to every other commentator on TV. I declined.*

Sports Commentators

With the advent of television, the role of a sports commentator has become increasingly blurred. TV is not by any sense of the imagination a new phenomenon, but commentators from virtually every sport seem to have forgotten the fundamentals of their role.

Originally there was radio, and the function of commentators was simple. They had to tell us listeners about something we couldn't see but they could. They had to try to paint a picture as accurately and excitingly as possible – a word picture of what was happening in the game being commentated on. They had to keep updating the score and make sure that we knew which individual player was being spoken about.

But commentating on TV is completely different. Now the job is to tell us about something *we* are seeing at the same time that the commentator is seeing it. We now need to be told something we don't know or something additional to what we are seeing in order to enrich the experience. We need to be informed and have interpreted what is happening in front of us, or even about something off-screen that we aren't seeing. Well, if that's their job, you could have fooled me.

How many times have you watched a soccer game and had to endure some halfwit telling you exactly what you are seeing? *'Ah, he has just passed to Rooney, oh, and Rooney has given it back to him, and now he crosses it ...'* Well I never, and there I was thinking he had just passed the ball to Rooney and Rooney had passed it back to him, and he crossed it.

It's not something that is exclusive to soccer. Cricket commentators are in a class of their own. *'And it's going all the way – yup, it's four runs to Smith.'* Well, thanks for that! I stupidly thought Smith had hit a four. Or, *'If only he would bowl a proper line and length, he would put more pressure on the batsman,'* said in the tone of someone delivering an oracle to the masses. Oh, I get it. If he bowls better, he will give the batsman more trouble? Fascinating! I wish I had thought of that.

But it is not only the banal statements of the obvious that are so frustrating. What about when they draw those classically inane conclusions along the lines of, *'Arsenal are going to have to score another goal if they want to win this match'*? This when the score is 1-1. *Really*?

Rugby also has its moments. *'It's over, and the flags go up ...'* Yes, it is, and yes, they do – and your point is? I don't doubt for a moment it is difficult to keep coming up with original, interesting facts and interpretations of what is happening on the field, but TV commentators don't *have* to talk the whole time. Commentating on a game like rugby, because the rules (especially around the scrum) are very complex and also constantly evolving, a knowledgeable commentator should always have lots to talk about.

When commentators are going to state the obvious, I appreciate it if they do so in original fashion. Like the ex-All Black rugby-legend-turned-commentator who, when describing an obviously very quick player, says, *'Look at him go – he's really got the wheels!'* Isn't that so much more descriptive than *'Boy, he is fast!'*? Or when describing a cleverly scored try: *'He went over as smooth as a Brazilian.'* And he isn't talking about someone from South America.

Perhaps the proper way to commentate for television is the method adopted by the South American soccer commentators. They get so excited and shout and scream so much that it is completely impossible to hear what they are saying. But from the electric, emotional mayhem and excitement they generate, you immediately know something wonderful is happening and you must be seeing a great game.

Football Traveller magazine, February 2009

24

Burglary

From 2004, Joost started developing a persecution complex. 'I had never had a problem with SARS [South African Revenue Service], nor had Amor, but suddenly they contacted both of us and told us they were going to do an audit. Which they did, and they found nothing!' He smiles triumphantly.

Joost was later told that SARFU had sent SARS a letter listing the names of about 10 Springbok rugby players – 'All of those who were given contracts after the 1995 World Cup.' Says Joost, 'I can't explain why they would have done it – but I know that SARFU had sent the letter. My source was impeccable. And let me phrase this as a question: Assuming they had sent it, who would have signed off on such a letter from SARFU? Obviously the president of SARFU, Brian van Rooyen,' he says, answering his own question.

When it's pointed out that a tax audit hardly adds up to persecution, Joost responds, 'Yeah, but a lot of things seem to have happened from 2004 onwards that don't always add up.'

During 2005, Joost and Amor decided to move from Silver Lakes in Pretoria to Johannesburg, as Joost had to commute to the City of Gold every day and Amor's studio was there too.

'We very quickly found a house in Dainfern Valley,' says Joost, 'which was ideal for our commuting requirements, and it was also the type of house we were looking for.'

Having lived in Pretoria for 35 years, and having often resisted criticism of the place as a country all on its own, Joost was amazed to find how different his new environment was.

'In Pretoria, if Amor and I went out for dinner, it became a "signing" session. If I went anywhere for a drink, everybody wanted to talk to me. But the stupid thing is that I thought that was the norm; that it was the price I had to pay for being famous. However, in Johannesburg it was completely different. People still acknowledged us, but they gave us much more space.'

To Joost it seemed as if Joburg people were less caught up in his and Amor's lives. The obvious explanation, of course, is that Pretoria is Blue Bulls country, and Joost is a legendary Blue Bull.

Interview with Joost van der Westhuizen

You were the Blue Bulls' favourite son. What was that like?
Well, my wife and I never went out for dinner, because it would always become a signing session. Same thing if we went shopping. We didn't mind when it happened, because it was our choice. But now that we live in Johannesburg, I find people respect our privacy far more. When they greet us they have manners and they don't cramp our space. So now I can see how claustrophobic it was in Pretoria.

The Weekender, 21–22 March 2009

'The exciting part,' he says, smiling, 'is that Amor was seven months pregnant with Kylie [at the time of the move]. Apparently moving house is right up there with the most stressful events in one's life, like death and divorce. So relocating from Pretoria to Johannesburg at that particular period, with a pregnant wife, was not the best timing in the world.'

A few months before moving to Dainfern, while still living at Silver Lakes, Amor awoke one night in a state of panic. At first she thought she had dreamt that there were people trying to break into their house, but after a few seconds she realised that there really were strange noises emanating from downstairs. Startled, she shook Joost and said, 'Shhhh … there are people in the house downstairs.'

Tired and half-asleep, Joost hoped Amor had been dreaming. But when she kept shaking him, he thought he had better get up and investigate.

Joost fetched his gun from the safe and motioned to Amor to press the panic button. Then he locked the bedroom door behind him and quietly made his way downstairs.

When he got to the lounge, across the room from where he was standing in the dark, he saw the silhouette of someone at one of the windows. Joost kept absolutely still. Then he became aware of a second person standing behind the first.

Joost's older brother Pieter had been in the police (where he had won a silver medal for bravery) and had on occasion given Joost advice on what to do if he ever found himself in this sort of situation.

Joost recalled Pieter telling him never to shoot at someone running away and, conversely, if he was going to shoot at someone attacking him, to aim at the body or the legs and not the head, as would be one's natural inclination.

At that point the shadowy figures managed to get the window open, as houses on a 'secure' estate such as Silver Lakes don't generally have burglar bars. Only one of the people outside climbed through the now open window, probably so that he could pass stuff to his accomplice waiting outside.

The intruder walked into and across the room to almost precisely where Joost was standing. While he appeared in the half-light to scan the place, Joost stepped out, pointed the gun at him and screamed, 'Stop!'

Without a nanosecond's hesitation, the intruder whirled around and took off through the window he had just come in. Completely forgetting Pieter's advice not to shoot at someone running away, Joost fired a shot but, selectively cognisant of his brother's other advice, made a point of aiming at the fleeing villain's legs. 'I hit the couch a beaut,' laughs Joost. He then flew through the window after the 'would-be' robber.

'I just went *bossies*.' An unbelievable physical chase ensued – over a wall, across a neighbouring stand that was still being developed and had building materials lying everywhere (Joost was barefoot and in his boxer shorts) and onto the golf course, the former world-class scrumhalf relentlessly pursued the rapidly tiring miscreant.

Eventually, after what seemed an absolute age, Joost brought down the escaping figure at the end of the fairway that ran adjacent to his house. In an absolute rage he rained blows down on what had turned out to be an exhausted black youth.

Shortly thereafter the estate's security, summoned when Amor had pressed the panic button in the bedroom, arrived to rescue the by-now bloodied, beleaguered, frightened and extremely unhappy burglar.

Months later, when the case went to court, Joost was astonished to find that far from being an ill-educated yob, 'the accused', as the putative thief was being referred to, was a presentable, eloquent young man who obviously fancied his chances as a lawyer, because he was representing himself.

His defence was that the story of the break-in was a complete fabrication on the part of the Van der Westhuizens. His version was that he was taking a quiet, late-night stroll on the golf course when he was attacked by the violent Joost.

Completely aghast at the turn of events, Joost eventually found himself in the witness box 'being cross-examined by the self-same bastard who, just a few months earlier, had stood in the dark of my lounge intending to rob me!'

The accused asked Joost a few irritating questions, one of which was, 'Did your house have a sign on it saying intruders were not allowed?'

The inanity of the question threw Joost for a second. 'Well, if that is what is worrying you, there is a sign at the entrance to the estate that says trespassers will be prosecuted, and you were trespassing.'

Unperturbed, the accused said to Joost, 'You claim there were two people trying to break in at your house ...'

Before he could finish wherever he was going with his line of questioning, Joost snapped at him, 'Well, if there weren't two, how many were there?'

Involuntarily, and obviously before giving the question much thought, the accused smugly replied, 'There was only one. I was on my own ...'

The courtroom, after an initial amazed silence, erupted in laughter as the now-befuddled accused blusteringly tried to distance himself from his own fatal admission. It was all to no avail.

His pretentious little charade of playing at being a lawyer had seriously backfired, and the obviously irritated magistrate imposed the maximum sentence he was allowed to hand down under the circumstances. The young 'bastard', as Joost referred to him, was sentenced to five years in jail and, before he could blink, bundled off to the cells below the court.

25

Strictly Come Dancing, a family feud and the Dainfern boom

At the end of 2006, Joost got a call from the producers of the popular television show *Strictly Come Dancing* to see if he would participate in a one-off edition of the show. The episode was to be recorded in December and then flighted on New Year's Eve. 'It was the Twenty20 of dancing,' laughs Joost. 'Everything would take place on the one night. It was not the normal, complete series.'

His 'opponents' were stand-up comedian Marc Lottering and dancer Sonja Stanford; actress and singer Sonja Herholdt and dancer Anthony Krotz; and TV presenter Claire Mawisa and dancer Brandon Eilers. Joost's partner and coach was the lovely Hayley Bennett. Smiling, Joost finds it necessary to mention that 'it was strictly dancing with Hayley'.

Each couple had to perform two dances from the *Strictly Come Dancing* selection: the tango, quickstep, foxtrot, waltz, jive, rumba, cha-cha and paso doble.

Joost had about three weeks to prepare. 'They suggested that I should train for around five hours a day, but I couldn't give up that much of my time, so I did an hour, three times a week.' When pressed, Joost confesses that Amor, who is a modern-dancing champion and has done all levels of Latin and ballroom dancing, helped him.

All went well for the intrepid rugby legend until the dress

rehearsal at the Carlton Centre. Joost and Hayley were due to perform a paso doble. Their opening move involved the apparently athletic Joost leaping off and down from a staircase. 'As a pretend sort-of bullfighter,' he explains.

A week before, Joost had been fitted out with a pair of flimsy Latin dance shoes. They weren't nearly as rugged as the boots he had worn when he played rugby. 'I leapt into the air in my new lightweight footwear, only to land and twist my ankle.'

Fortunately, being a veteran of a million rugby games, Joost knew something about sports injuries. He iced his ankle and then strapped the offending joint. Joost mentions that as a former Springbok rugby player and supposedly tough guy, he felt acutely embarrassed at the possibility that he might not be able to continue with the show.

'I could just hear Marc Lottering telling the audience at his next show how I got injured during *Strictly Come Dancing* ...

'I couldn't believe it – we were an hour away from the recording of the actual show and here I was, Mr Rough-Tough-Rugby-Player, injured! I thought, bugger it, I'm going to jump again.' He laughs loudly at the thought. Fortunately, the next leap went off without a hitch.

Later, after the rehearsal, to his surprise but absolute delight, the well-strapped former Springbok scrumhalf and his dancing coach went on to win the competition.

'I really enjoyed it, I must say. It was such fun. I've got my trophy at home,' he smiles proudly.

'When I started doing well in rugby,' says Joost, 'I realised that I wasn't spending any time with people who weren't involved in the sport. So I started organising a golf day for my close friends. Everything was on me – I paid for the lot. We called it the J9 Invitational. The first year there were only about eight of us. Anyway, it went on and grew in numbers until, in 2007, there must have been 24 people playing.'

By this stage Joost had managed to organise sponsors for various aspects of his golf day. 'I arranged a bus that was paid for by a company and sponsors gave us golf shirts and prizes.'

In 2007, the venue was the Bronkhorstspruit golf course. Joost's group had only played three holes when their game was rained out and everyone adjourned to the pub. After a few drinks, it was decided to go to one of Joost's friend's houses for the prize-giving.

Before the men left the pub at the golf club, Joost saw his younger brother, Gustav, talking to one of his oldest friends, Nico. Neither looked very happy. On the way out, Joost asked his friend what the problem was. Nico looked at him and said, 'Remember where you come from?'

'What do you mean?' said Joost, taken aback.

'I've been talking to Gustav, and apparently you never see your family any more.' This irritated Joost, but he left it, as everyone was moving to the new venue.

When Joost got to his friend's house, he asked his dad if he would sort things out with his brother, as he didn't want to spoil the day by getting into an internecine argument.

However, when his dad came back from talking to Gustav, to Joost's astonishment he said it was necessary for Joost to spend more time with his family. This from a father he called every single day.

At that point, Joost lost it. 'If your lives revolve around me, then just get out of my life. Maybe if I'm not in your lives, you can get on with yours. Why don't you all just go and get stuffed.' With that, his dad and two brothers left immediately. For Joost, the whole day was irreparably spoilt.

'The problem was,' says Joost, 'the next day was my mother's birthday. So I phoned her that evening and told her my family would not be attending her lunch. Shame. She just cried. My mom is an angel and she didn't need this crap in her life. But we didn't go to her birthday lunch. Actually I was in the wrong, because the fight had nothing to do with her.'

The problem, it emerged, had arisen during a holiday at the coast. Every year Joost and Amor took turns to invite their respective families to join them at their cottage at Keurboomstrand. One year Gustav had a fight with Amor when she asked him to help tidy up. He thought she was implying that he and, for some unclear reason, his father were lazy.

For a long time after the golf-day incident, Joost and Gustav didn't speak to each other unless it was absolutely necessary. Sadly for his friends, the feud also heralded the demise of the annual golf day. (After Joost's collapse in 2009, discussed later, Gustav and Joost mended their relationship.)

When I speak to Joost's father, it becomes apparent that there might be another side to the story. It seems that between 2004 and 2007, Joost had not yet shaken his infamous arrogance and sense of self-importance, fuelled by years of adulation from his multitude of fans.

Joost was quite capable of cancelling arrangements at the last minute, but Gustav Sr won't elaborate other than to mention that he always had a back-up organised when he was supposed to play golf with his son. This was just in case Joost phoned at the last minute to cancel, usually without explanation. However, Gustav is at pains to stress that this no longer happens.

'We played recently and Joost was fantastic. He arrived early and talked to everyone. It was just like old times,' says his proud father.

His mother, the very dignified Mariana, simply observes that she thinks that, for a while at least, Joost forgot who he was and where he came from.

Dainfern is an upmarket, high-security gated suburb to the north of Sandton. It lies incongruously alongside and below a huge silver sewage pipe that crosses the valley in which the estate is situated. Squinting at the intrusive pipe through one eye in the half-light and from a long way away while wearing dark glasses, it bears a vague resemblance to a Roman aqueduct. In the cold, clear light of day, it is simply hideous.

The security personnel at Dainfern are notorious for their obdurateness, and the measures employed to protect the inhabitants make the security arrangements at Fort Knox pale in comparison. Apart from a massive fence, there are two electronically boomed entrances complete with enormous gatehouses – one on the east side, close to Joost's home, and one on the west side.

Both are manned by a squad of security guards that insist on IDs, driver's licences, birth certificates, family trees, references, marriage certificates, divorce papers, rates bills and verified appointments before allowing access to visitors.

Joost lives on the east side of Dainfern, in the neighbouring suburb of Dainfern Valley. In 2008, Amor enrolled their four-year-old son Jordan at a soccer club called the Mud Puppies, which was situated in Dainfern.

Joost is of the belief that there are cross-training benefits between most sports, and so he fully supported his little boy playing a game he hadn't, till then, had much to do with. However, Amor's father, Jordan's *nonno* (Italian for grandfather), had been a professional soccer player.

Jordan loved his first training session. While running around in his track shoes, he soon noticed, however, that all the other boys had proper football boots. '*Pa, ek wil sulke skoene hê, asseblief.*'

'Of course I'll buy them for you, my boy,' promised Joost. He still remembered how his rugby boots were stolen from the family car when he was small and his dad, despite not being able to afford them, immediately went and got him a new pair. 'Ah, my chance to do it for my son,' he thought sentimentally.

The following Wednesday, when Jordan was due to have his second training session with the Mud Puppies, Joost frantically drove from sports shop to sports shop, looking for a pair of minute football boots. Finally, he found some right across town.

'I was having a meeting in the south, and in desperation I

popped into a store there. Fortunately they had a pair that was the right size. By that stage I was frantic that I was going to let my son down.'

Late, but thrilled that he had kept his promise, Joost, because he was returning from the south instead of using the entrance closest to his home, raced down Cedar Road in the new black Audi RS4 he had just collected from the dealers, towards Dainfern's west entrance.

'Where are you going to?' asked the female security guard. Somewhat gratuitously Joost mentions that she was fat.

'To watch my boy play soccer at the Mud Puppies,' Joost cheerfully replied.

'You don't live in Dainfern,' she said, stating the blindingly obvious.

If he was a resident, why would he be at the visitor's entrance, wondered Joost. Then he made a mistake.

'No,' he said, 'I live across in Dainfern Valley.'

'Oh, I know you guys – you just want to take a short cut.'

A somewhat taken-aback Joost said, 'Look, here are my son's new soccer boots. Please, I'm late and he's waiting for them.'

At this juncture the guard asked to see Joost's driver's licence. As seems to be inevitable in situations where a person in a peaked cap is pulling rank, the vital document is never where it should be. Damn! Joost thought. He had left his wallet containing his licence in his wife's car. Trying to explain this to the inflexible, portly protector of the wealthy Dainfern residents was like trying to push toothpaste back into the tube.

'My licence is with my wife down at the fields. Let me go in and drop off the boots, and I'll bring it back to show you.'

'You can't go in.'

After arguing with the intractable security guard for a few more moments, the by-then completely exasperated Joost asked if he could see her supervisor. The security manager was called and reluctantly came out to see what the fuss was about. Also female and also gratuitously overweight, she took one look at Joost and irrationally said, 'No, he can't go in – he's full of shit.'

At this point, Joost walked over to the boom and lifted it. 'One-handed – you can see it on their security film,' he says. And then he climbed back into his new vehicle and drove through.

He had hardly got a car's-length into the estate when the cavalry, in the form of a security car containing two guards, arrived. 'I immediately pulled over,' he says. 'You can also see that in their film.'

For the umpteenth time Joost explained his soccer-boot predicament to the fortunately more receptive mobile guards who, without any hassle, agreed to accompany him down to the field. The senior of the two smiled and said to Joost, 'Those women are full of shit. We'll go with you.'

Joost got to the field and rushed to find a despairing Jordan, who was about to kick off, and gave him the boots. 'He was so happy. That little face – I will never forget his smile for the rest of my life.'

After the game, Joost went to the security office in the centre of the estate to explain to the über–security manager what had happened. He again clarified what his situation vis-à-vis Jordan and the boots had been and, biting his tongue, apologised for losing his cool. He even offered to pay for any damages. At one stage he categorically said to the guy, 'I'm sorry, I was wrong.'

'No problem,' the security manager said; they would contact him.

The next day the manager's manager, a Mr Gerald Plots, phoned Joost and requested a meeting. He told Joost he would assess the damage and send him an invoice. 'We needed a meeting for something that had effectively been settled the afternoon of the incident?' asks Joost indignantly.

The mind boggles to think how much energy was being expended on what was, in fact, a storm in a teacup. Presumably the security at Dainfern exists to keep miscreants out and to stop it becoming a thoroughfare to other suburbs. That they were now relentlessly pursuing the father of a little boy who played soccer in their precinct confounded Joost.

But it didn't end there. 'Eight days later, I got a call from the Douglasdale police station saying I should come and see them. They wanted to arrest me for trespassing and for breaking the boom at Dainfern West gate.' An angry Joost politely suggested that as he was a taxpayer he had the right to be arrested at home, so they had better come and fetch him.

Curiouser and curiouser. The next day, while driving the kids to school, Joost heard a police spokesman being interviewed on the *Breakfast Show*, saying that Mr van der Westhuizen had broken the boom at Dainfern 'with his bare hands'. This was undoubtedly added to make the listeners aware of just how heinous a crime it really was. (Presumably if Joost had smashed the boom with a crowbar it would have been a mitigating factor.)

The exact transcript of the piece on the radio goes as follows:

Joost van der Westhuizen could find himself behind bars soon for malicious damage to property and trespassing. A case was opened against the former Springbok captain earlier this week after he allegedly broke a boom gate at the Dainfern Golf Estate in Northern Johannesburg last Wednesday. Authorities say Van der Westhuizen became agitated when security guards at the gate refused to let him enter because he didn't have any form of identification. Here is the police's Bulani Mutane: 'Mr van der Westhuizen had an argument with the security then went to the boom. He broke the boom with his bare hands and got back to his vehicle and showed the security his middle finger and drove through ...'

Joost got home to a furious Amor. She had listened to the same radio station. 'How could you behave like that?' she snapped at him.

'I didn't!' yelled Joost. 'Has everyone gone mad?'

He immediately tried to arrange a meeting with Dainfern über-über-management. Three days later, he finally met with the estate manager, the security manager and one other to watch the security film. The film was quite clear, but there was no sound. On inquiring about the sound, Joost was told that it hadn't been working at the time of the incident. 'Very convenient,' said Joost. 'Now we can't hear what your guards were saying to me.'

An aggravating aspect of the whole debacle was that Dainfern kept saying Joost's car was illegal because it didn't have number plates. 'But it had a permit stuck on the back windscreen,' says an irate Joost. 'Did they bother to look? Not a fuck! If it was illegal, it was the garage's fault. I'd just collected the car – I assumed they knew what paperwork was required to drive it legally. Apart from anything, what did my car's legality have to do with Dainfern?'

The film didn't help Joost, because the security guards couldn't be heard refusing him admission. Nor could his requests to go and collect his licence from his wife at the Mud Puppies be heard. Then, to crown everything, they handed Joost not an invoice, but a quotation for R15 000.

—- Original Message —-
From: gerald
To: 'Joost'
Sent: Thursday, May 08, 2008 12:38 PM
Subject: Boom gate

Dear Mr van der Westhuizen,
I acknowledge receipt of your email dated 7 May 2008 and wish to respond as follows:
1. As far as Dainfern Golf and Residential Estate are concerned the matter regarding the incident which occurred on the 16 April 2008 has now been closed.

2. The incident was reported at the Douglasdale Police Station and the case no is 634-04-2008.
3. You are most welcome to the damaged parts (internal mechanism). We can make arrangements for you to collect same.
4. The camera footage and files relating to the incident remains the property of Dainfern Estate and will not be released to any outside sources.
5. A copy of the Quotation for the repairs to the Boom Gate is attached.

Regards

Gerald Plots

Estate Manager

Dainfern Golf and Residential Estate

PROVICOM ELECTRONICS QUOTATION

DAINFERN EST				18 April 2008	
QUOTE FOR BOOM DAMAGED BY J VAN DE WESTHUIZEN				QUOTE SJ 221	
		ATT: GEARLD			
ITEM NO.	PART NO.	DESCRIPTION	QTY	PRICE	TOTAL
		EQUIPMENT			
1		CO MPLETE BOOM EXCLUDING ARM	1	12430.00	12430.00
2		3M OCTO BOOM ARM	1	922.00	922.00
		SYSTEM TOTAL NETT			13352.00
		TOTAL VAT 14%			1869.28
		TOTAL INCLUDING VAT			15221.28
		EXCLUDES ANY OTHER COST THAT MAY ARISE DURING INSTALLATION/REPAIRS			
		VALIDITY OF QUOTE 5 DAYS			
		CONDITIONS			
		1. OUR STANDARD CONDITIONS OF SALE APPLY			
		2. NO PURCHASES WILL BE ACCEPTED WITHOUT AN OFFICIAL ORDER			
		3. A 10% HANDLING FEE WILL BE LEVIED ON GOODS RETURNED FOR CREDIT			
		4. SOILED GOODS WILL NOT BE ACCEPTED BACK FOR CREDIT			
		5. PRICES ARE BASED ON CURRENT EXCHANGE RATES AND DUTIES			
		6. PRICES ARE SUBJECT TO CHANGE WITHOUT PRIOR NOTICE			
		7. GOODS REMAIN THE PROPERTY OF PROVICOM UNTIL PAID FOR IN FULL			

Later, when the dust had settled, Joost investigated what a gate cost. 'A new gate, motor and a boom – a three-metre boom – cost R7 000. There was no damage to the boom. I lifted it with my bare hands – what could have happened to it? So where did they get R15 000?

Also, I phoned the guy who had the security tender there. He told me I had only broken a gear on the boom motor, which cost in the region of R3 000 to repair. Strangely, when I phoned him a second time to get that in writing, he said he wasn't *allowed* to talk to me.'

Joost shook his head. 'I had to pay the 15 grand to get the charges dropped and for my boy to be allowed to keep going into Dainfern to play with the Mud Puppies. Going to court would just have been nuisance value and have cost me the same in the end. Getting arrested wasn't an option. Interestingly, when I now take Jordan to soccer, all the guards know my name and they are all pleased to see me – so you tell me what it was all about?'

Answering his own question, he says resentfully, 'It's the name "Joost van der Westhuizen". You would think because I was well known I wouldn't have been a danger to the residents of Dainfern. Instead, I just became a means of generating publicity for them. The story was in all the newspapers and on all the radio stations and they put the incident in their monthly newsletter, where they talked of discovering an intruder on the estate and he was the well-known former rugby player Mr Joost van der Westhuizen! Me, a bloody intruder? And they "discovered" me? I was at their fucking gate trying to get in!'

When Joost is reminded that the whole thing had not been a complete disaster, as he had managed to keep his promise to his son and keep alive the Van der Westhuizen tradition of success-fully resolving boot crises, he laughs.

'Jordan's tiny boots were a bloody lot more expensive than mine ever were.'

26

Writing Joost's book VI

Listening to Joost talk about his confrontation with Dainfern security, I feel my blood begin to boil. I, too, have had a couple of run-ins with the bad-mannered and ill-tempered guards who man their gates. I have no issue with the principle of booming off suburbs and protecting the residents, but what annoys is when it is no longer an exercise in security but in persecution.

So, when Joost tells me about his fight with his father and brothers, I find myself sympathising. Gosh, we're really bonding!

My current ex-wife was a professional tennis player, and through her I met numerous famous people. I am talking about really famous people – names like John McEnroe, Björn Borg, Martina Navratilova, Chris Evert, Jack Nicholson, James Hunt and many others. It was fascinating to observe how everyone around them – friends, family and even casual acquaintances – all wanted a piece of their particular star.

I'm not sure whether they believe that there is some kind of spin-off for them in being seen with a superstar – some sort of fame by association – or whether it is simply because these people lead boring, mundane lives that they need to live vicariously through someone else, as Joost has accused his family of doing. Joost, it seems, was having enough difficulty being arrogant, good-looking, rich and famous; he certainly didn't need the added pressure of living on their behalf.

Pondering the issue, it probably partly explains the popularity of the scandal magazines that so delight in exposing celebrities' flaws in general, and in making Joost and Amor's life so miserable in par-

ticular. *Perhaps people want to know all the dirt on the stars because it makes their own shabby little lives seem more bearable.*

'Fortunately,' I say to him, 'Amor is probably even more famous than you, so you don't have the fame-by-association syndrome to deal with in your relationship.'

Joost is in a bad mood and not to be distracted by my theories. 'Funny how these articles about the bloody video and how shocking it is are continually appearing, but have you seen one single piece about the people who made the video and how many laws they broke? Entrapment, blackmail, defamation, drug use — you name it, they are definitely guilty of breaking a number of laws. But has anyone been arrested? Has anyone been charged?'

He then delivers a five-minute diatribe on how the press in this country has completely lost any moral compass. I'm surprised at his eloquence and also at his assumption that the press had ever been moral. Unfortunately politeness, decency and accuracy have never sold newspapers. Good news is not generally interesting. People would rather hear how the one-armed tattooed lesbian murdered her live-in lover by pouring acid over her while she was sleeping, robbed a bank and ran away with a child she groomed on the internet than how some good Samaritan bought a beggar a wheelchair.

'In a proper country, they would have jailed that scum by now,' Joost continues, 'regardless of whether I was going to sue or not. Although, when you think about it, there's no point in suing the people who made the video, because they are lowlives who don't have any money.' Curiously, he doesn't mention suing the magazines or newspapers ... hmmm.

I am interested in finding out what a dyed-in-the-wool South-African like Joost van der Westhuizen thinks a 'proper' country is, but I remember that we have work to do. I assume that on his way to meet me he was assailed by yet another headline shouting his name. I suggest to my NBF that we have a beer and leave the entire video situation until later.

In any event, I'm not wearing any socks.

Joost arrives at our next meeting wanting to know where I was 14 years ago. When I look blank, he repeats, 'Where were you on 24 June, 14 years ago?'

'Oh, yes – at the final of the 1995 Rugby World Cup ...' No sooner do I answer than his phone rings. It is François Pienaar, wishing Joost happy memories of that eventful day. Joost chats for a few moments. He then hands the phone to me so that I can say hello to the former Springbok captain. I remind François that we met on 22 November 2008, outside the suites' entrance at Twickenham after the Springboks had thrashed England 42-6.

That evening, while we stood outside the giant stadium chatting, a very attractive young girl recognised the former Springbok captain and came up to ask for his autograph. She was wearing next to nothing in the cool weather, but fortunately seemed alcoholically immunised against the chill. She handed François a Koki pen and said, 'Sign.'

'Where?' François asked.

'Here,' she said, lifting her already tiny little top almost over her head with her one hand and pointing with the other at her gorgeous, unblemished, perfectly flat, tanned tummy.

François smiled at me and gently, near her belly-button, drew a neat little X, which he circled. The girl looked down at his handi-work; then, with a huge smile, gave us both a thumbs-up and François a kiss on his cheek, and staggered off.

The moment I remind him where we met, François laughs and says, 'How was that tummy?' He remembers ...

It seems it is a day for phone calls. No sooner has François rung off than Joost's phone rings again. The call is from Breyton Paulse. He just wants to know how Joost is and when they can get together.

We proceed to work and Joost tells me bizarre tales of blackmail and other nefarious happenings. I observe that he seems to be a walk-ing magnet for villains.

27

Blackmail

'About halfway through 2006,' says Joost, 'I participated in a golf day at the Carousel (a casino 55 kilometres north of Pretoria). We played at Elements Golf Club, west of Warmbaths.'

While there, Joost received a phone call that displayed as a private number on his cellphone. Joost took the call.

A guttural Afrikaans voice came on the line and said, 'We want you to pay us some money. We know where you live, we know what your kids look like – we know everything about you. Don't, whatever you do, go to the police.' Then the line went dead.

Joost was bemused but didn't do anything, not wanting to get hysterical because of one phone call. He also had a fleeting thought that it might be one of his mates pulling his leg – which, if it was, wasn't very funny. He put the call out of his head.

But then, the next day, the same guy called and said that 'they' wanted half-a-million rand. When asked what they had to offer in return, Joost replies, 'My family's safety.'

He goes on: 'When you suddenly find yourself in such an obscure, weird, unbelievable and very frightening situation, and it is your family who is being threatened, you certainly don't think clearly.

'I simply didn't know what to do. It was just straight bloody blackmail.'

Joost then contacted someone, whom he would rather not name, who was involved in police intelligence. This person instructed Joost to buy some time by telling the blackmailers that he would pay them, but that he had to transfer the money from

England and the transaction had to be cleared by the Reserve Bank. He would need time.

When the next call came, Joost said exactly what he had been instructed to say.

A few days later, in the early evening, Joost received a chilling phone call in which he could hear Amor singing in the background at some function. The same guttural voice said, 'I can see you aren't here, nor are your kids, but your wife certainly is – listen.'

Joost got hold of his contact and said, 'You have to do something. This is getting out of hand.'

Joost and his contact checked his and Amor's diaries and found that the two of them would be performing at a function together in the near future – she would be singing and he handing out prizes – at Centurion Park. Joost and his man hatched a plan.

When the blackmailer next called, Joost told him to come to Centurion Park on the night he and Amor would be performing. Joost said he would be in his silver BMW X5. A suitcase of money would be left in the boot and the car would be left unlocked. Joost insisted that the blackmailer arrive at 8.30 p.m. sharp, or else he would have to send his brother to arrange the exchange.

The conversation then took a surreal turn. The voice said, 'Which brother, older or younger?'

Not surprised that the man knew he had two brothers, Joost asked, 'What difference does it make?'

The voice replied that he had played rugby with Joost's younger brother Gustav. Joost then knew someone in the rugby fraternity was involved.

The pickup didn't go according to plan. At the appointed time, from where he was stationed inside the building, Joost could see a person walking towards his car. At the last moment, as the man neared Joost's vehicle, he took fright for some reason and jumped into a vehicle that seemed to appear out of nowhere, which took off at high speed. Immediately cars sprang into action all around and gave chase.

Completely unaware of events, Amor, having finished her set, walked into the middle of all the excitement. It took a while, but eventually she was fully apprised of the whole grubby situation.

She responded by visibly experiencing the whole gamut of emotions. Alternately angry, frightened, sad, tearful, hysterical and terrified, she was ultimately just relieved.

Joost had been acting strangely the past couple of months and had been making and receiving clandestine phone calls; there had also been unexplained absences, and Amor had started to think that Joost was having an affair. The truth now revealed the reasons for his odd behaviour.

This peculiar narrative then becomes even murkier. According to Joost's contact, the blackmailers were caught that night and were in jail. But without a court case? Joost didn't quite understand. Without his laying charges and the normal legal rigmarole, how could they be in jail? When he pushed for further explanations, his contact said, 'Look, it's been taken care of. I give you my word – they will never bother you again.'

Rather irrationally, Joost decided to accept his contact's assurances. He was so relieved that the inexplicable, horrible little drama had come to an end without his family being hurt and without the loss of money that he was happy to let it die a quiet death. And, knowing his contact as he did and the shadowy world he inhabited, he secretly suspected some other form of punishment had been visited on the perpetrators.

Since the dramatic night at Centurion Park, and without ever having found out exactly what had happened or knowing why he had been targeted, or daring to think about what might have transpired had he rejected the blackmailer's demands, Joost has not heard another word from the man with the guttural voice.

28

Tukkies

In 2006, Joost van der Westhuizen was invited to be the technical director of rugby coaching at Pretoria University. As he grew familiar with the mechanics of his new position, Joost decided if bureaucracy ever became an Olympic event, the Tuks Rugby Club would definitely finish on the podium. As he diligently battled his way through a morass of ineffective and dysfunctional structures, he couldn't help but be amazed that things were in such a mess at a place of higher learning. Then, just when he thought he had seen it all, he experienced first-hand the entrenched system of line management that was in operation at the university.

It worked like this: Joost would put in a request for a change in procedures to his line manager. His line manager would pass Joost's request on to another, more senior individual, who in turn would give it to his boss. That boss would undertake, the minute he returned from leave/conference/bosberaad/international convention/team-building exercise/funeral, to submit the request to his superior, whose job was to brief the head of department.

The head of department would then arrange for the board to convene to consider whether or not to table the request. The board's decision would be passed on to the dean for ratification, and his signature. Of course, at no point did anyone in the chain of command think of advising Joost on the status of his request; it wasn't their job. (Obviously this was not what it was really like – to Joost, it only felt that way ...)

'Despite the game having turned professional,' says Joost, 'what struck me was just how truly amateur the clubs were.'

He realised that if Tuks was to survive in club rugby, certain business structures and procedures would have to be implemented. The procedure up till then had been for the rugby club to take receipt of their annual budget, which they would then spend; if any money was left over, they would declare a profit. Innovatively they tried to limit the spending in order to ensure profitability.

To his astonishment, Joost also discovered that 19 students on rugby bursaries at the university didn't actually play rugby. 'Nobody ran checks and there were no structures in place. I was expecting at any moment to discover that we also had girls on rugby bursaries – maybe some hookers?' he laughs. 'Nothing would have surprised me.'

After six months of adhering to the line-management structure, putting forward business proposals and getting no response, Joost jumped the queue and went directly to see the dean of the university, Kallie Pistorius. 'He was fantastic. Within a month of the meeting, he gave us half a million out of his own budget.'

It made a huge difference to Joost's job. He could pay the players' expenses and introduce incentives for them, which obviously made playing for the club more appealing.

'We could now offer more bursaries to talented players coming through from the schools. And this time we made sure that the guys who got the bursaries played rugby,' he smiles. 'You can't believe what a difference just those small things made to the club. We started to win more games, attract more and better players, and there was a great spirit about the place.'

At the time Joost was at Tuks, the former Springbok eighth man and captain, Wynand Claassen, was chairman of the university's Rugby Supporters' Club, whose mission was to raise funds for the club.

'Unfortunately,' says Joost, 'no money ever seemed to be forthcoming. The one year they had ties made to celebrate the centenary of the University of Pretoria. Obviously, the intention was to sell those commemorative ties to raise funds. Instead, when all was said and done, the university ended up with a bill of R52 000 for the ties; ironic for a place where no one, except maybe the lecturers, wore ties.'

Joost seemed to spend his life bumping heads with Claassen. 'At one stage I suggested he change the name of his club to the Tuks Rugby Criticising Club. Because every time we asked them for money, they would respond by telling us how badly we were doing on the field.' Paradoxically, without exception, he says, the Supporters' Club members never attended any of the university's rugby games. 'So whoever came to watch games were not "supporters" in the official sense,' Joost smiles.

In a classic case of *Groundhog Day*, in three months the agenda for their monthly joint meetings never changed. 'All we did was alter the date on the programme; it was always the same points that had to be discussed. We just never seemed to make any progress and there was always a fight at those meetings. Funny, they would also regularly moan to me about not having sponsors, but wouldn't do anything about approaching companies to support us.'

The structure of club rugby at the time required that every team entered in the Carlton Cup League had to have a second team, an Under-20 team and a junior team. Because Tuks had two teams in the first league – their first team and a team called the Fezelas – effectively they needed to put out eight teams.

Joost's solution was to enter only one team in the Carlton Cup. This immediately gave the university a bigger pool of players from which to choose. 'Suddenly we were strong,' says Joost. 'Whereas before we had quantity in terms of teams, they were spread thin in terms of quality. Now we had quantity in terms of available players, because we had half the number of teams and, most importantly, we had quality.'

But Joost found his innovative ideas weren't always appreciated by everyone – particularly not by the archetypal rugby supporter Wynand Claassen. He was infuriated with Joost's decision. 'You are tampering with the foundations of Springbok rugby ('Bit presumptuous,' thought Joost) and messing with the traditions of the university,' Claassen declared angrily during one of their many fractious meetings.

Claassen's ally was the former Northern Transvaal player and incumbent president of Tuks Rugby Club, Dr Dawie Marais. 'He sent me a text message,' says Joost, 'saying that if I went ahead with my plans, I would always be remembered as the person who had destroyed the university's rugby club. These were the people I worked for – these were *my* "old farts".' (In the run-up to the 1995 Rugby World Cup, England captain Will Carling was briefly relieved of his post for calling the English RFU board members old farts.)

The proof in the pudding Joost baked at Tuks came at the end of the 2008 season, when Tukkies had a team in every final, and they lost in only one.

In fact, Tuks had become too strong for the Carlton Cup League; they started beating clubs like Eersterust by more than 100 points. Fortunately, First National Bank, in the form of François Pienaar, came forward as sponsors for the University Cup, a tournament played between the universities of Bloemfontein, Cape Town, Potchefstroom, Port Elizabeth, Pretoria, Stellenbosch and Johannesburg, and the Tswane University of Technology. 'It's the equivalent of Monday-night football in the States,' says Joost. In 2007, Tukkies lost in the semi-finals, and in 2008 they lost in the final.

After the match, the team and their director of coaching went into town to find a place to have a drink. While happily ensconced in a festive student watering hole, standing in a circle wallowing in a mixture of success at reaching the final and sorrow at losing it, a nondescript, scruffy individual who was standing behind Joost placed his head next to Joost's and asked, 'Are you Joost van der Westhuizen?' Joost smiled and nodded.

'Well, I think you're a cunt,' snarled the man.

'Thank you,' said Joost. 'A lot of people think I am.'

The scruffy one then walked around the circle of drinking Tuks players, who were unaware of what had just transpired. He would have been fine had he kept going, but instead the abusive fellow stopped, stuck his hand into the circle and, as a parting shot, gave Joost the finger and said, 'Fuck you!'

It was never established what had prompted the unpleasant interlude or even who the man was, because as Joost's abuser withdrew his arm, the player standing nearest the discourteous interloper turned, growled, 'Don't talk to my coach like that!' and smashed a fist into the man's face. Then all hell broke loose, as it often does when a punch is thrown in a crowded, alcoholic gathering.

As soon as he could, Joost got his men outside and told them to go back to their lodgings. 'Don't worry,' he assured them, 'I'll be fine and I'll sort out any problems with the management.'

By this stage the obnoxious perpetrator of the trouble was not feeling at all well. In the chaos that had ensued after the first punch, it seemed he was pretty thoroughly taken care of by Joost's players.

Joost found the pub manager and gave his version of events. He apologised for the mess and offered to pay for any damages. He then made his way back to his accommodation.

The next day the inevitable reports appeared in the press, blaming Joost for the trouble. Despite having had no involvement in the actual fisticuffs and having done his best to neutralise the fracas by getting his players out of the pub, the various newspapers roundly derided Joost for setting a bad example. Between Joost and the media, it was a case of 'a luta continua'.

It was during his tenure at Tuks that Joost had to deal with parents for the first time – usually fathers. Occasionally, there was also the odd man-eating mother to contend with. It seemed as if Joost's office was a magnet for a constant stream of angry, disillusioned, blindly optimistic and threateningly ambitious daddies

who wanted to know what he was doing with their darling off-
spring.

'It was amazing how often the reason they came to see me
generally had nothing to do with their sons. It was all about
the fathers' hopes and ambitions. They were trying to fulfil their
own dreams and ambitions through the careers of their kids.
When you got the boys on their own, you found that their goals
differed quite radically from their fathers' ideas of where they were
heading.'

Joost remembers one particular meeting with a father and son
in his office. After a brief chat about life in general, Joost asked
the boy what his goal in life was. The father answered, 'To be the
best rugby player he can be.' (The father had played representative
rugby.) Joost repeated his question to the son, but this time when
the father began to answer, Joost held up his hand and pointed
at the boy to respond.

'My dad says I should be ...'

'Start again,' Joost interrupted him. 'And this time leave off
the bit about "my dad says".'

Looking slightly sheepish, the boy said, 'Well, I'd like to be
the best I can be.'

'At what?' asked Joost.

'Uh, rugby ...' the son said, looking nervously at his father.
'Maybe flyhalf ...'

At this stage, the agitated father looked as if he was about to
say something. But before he could get a word out, Joost asked
the man to excuse them for a moment, as he wanted to talk to
the boy alone.

Reluctantly, the father left the room.

Joost smiled at the boy and said, 'Look, while it's just us here,
tell me what you really want. Not this wishy-washy "best you can
be". If you think about it – when you break it down – it doesn't
actually mean anything. Try to look ahead. What is your real goal
in life; what would you like to be? Be specific. For instance, do

you want to be a Springbok, or a Blue Bull? You must name it to claim it. It's all right to want what *you* want.'

It wasn't long before Joost and the boy found some answers that made sense to both of them. The father was readmitted to the room.

'Right,' said Joost to the young man. 'What would you like to be?'

With surprising confidence, no doubt prompted by the former Springbok's pep talk, the boy looked at his father and said firmly, 'I'd like to be the best criminal lawyer ever to come out of this university.'

On other occasions the fathers would want to know how much Joost was going to pay their sons.

'I'm not,' he would say.

'Nothing? But he has already been offered a contract by the technikon.'

'Well, why are you sitting here? Shouldn't you be at the technikon?'

When fathers became pushy about their sons being chosen for particular teams, Joost would say to them, 'So in effect you want me to pick him because you think he is good enough. What happens if I ever have to drop him? Will you stand by me then?'

Joost changed the way things were run from the basics upwards. In his first year at Tuks he would chase away latecomers to training. He demanded proper behaviour at all times when players were representing the rugby club and insisted that everyone greet everyone else.

The change, he says, was astonishing. 'When I first started, you couldn't believe the big-deal attitudes of some of the players. They could hardly find the energy to greet me. Half of them would arrive late for practice. When they walked off to go and change, I would ask, "Where do you think you're going?" When they said to change for practice, I told them that they weren't training that night, so they might as well leave. They knew that if they didn't train, they didn't play. It didn't take long,' he laughs, 'before I had wonderfully punctual players who all made a huge point of greeting their coach ...'

During 2008, Joost started looking for opportunities of a more commercial nature. To that end he wound down his involvement in Tuks rugby by delegating some of his functions to Jannie Robertse. 'I actually arranged for him to receive R10 000 a month of my salary, so as to compensate for the extra workload I was giving him,' says Joost.

In August of 2008, Joost gave notice of his intention to leave at the end of the year.

29

Progressive Investment Holdings

At the beginning of 2008, Joost met Freddie Andalaft, an ostensible financial services consultant with his own company, Progressive Investment Holdings (PIH). Freddie had hired Joost to MC a function for PIH at Finsure in Bloemfontein.

Not long after the function, Andalaft called and offered Joost a job with PIH. Apparently Freddie saw himself as a dealmaker, and he wanted a well-known person to be his CEO. When Joost explained that he knew very little about the industry and even less about being a CEO, Freddie said no problem, they would train him.

Eventually it was agreed that Joost would train for nine months and would then take over Freddie Andalaft's position. To this end, Freddie appointed Murray Kilgour, a life coach, to turn the former rugby star into CEO of PIH. Joost remembers that his first file was called 'How to become a CEO'.

In the beginning, all Joost had to do was attend meetings and study on his own. The company was situated in Bedfordview. Surprisingly, the offices were small and cramped.

'The first thing I did,' says Joost, 'was to try to understand the financial services vocabulary.' But he readily admits he was way out of his depth and not entirely convinced that he would be able to achieve what Freddie wanted.

When, after two months, Freddie unexpectedly called Joost in and started a lengthy explanation on how his previous company was being liquidated and that there were a few problems with business in general, Joost saw a way out and resigned on the spot. 'I told him that if the press got hold of it, it would do my name a lot of damage and I wasn't prepared to take that chance, so I was off.'

That was in May 2008. In total, Joost was at PIH for exactly two months. In December, reports appeared in various news-papers about the liquidation of the company. The headline of an article by Roy Cokayne in the *Star* newspaper on 10 December 2008 reads: 'Court tackles rugby star's investment group'. The first paragraph mentions Joost's name: 'A financial investment group that raised R100 million from investors through an allegedly unlawful scheme and had former rugby player Joost van der Westhuizen as its chief operating officer has been put in pro-visional liquidation.'

It doesn't appear again. Freddie Andalaft's name appears five times in the approximately 500-word article. Joost worked at PIH for two months; Freddie Andalaft founded, owned and ran PIH. But whose name appeared in the headlines? Also, Joost was never the chief operating officer – he was in training to be the CEO, an entirely different matter.

A few pages later, in the same edition of the *Star*, 'hidden' in a column titled 'Business Watch', the following sentence appears:

> There have not been any suggestions that Van der Westhuizen, who was learning the ropes with a view to becoming chief executive, next month, was involved in unlawful conduct.

Interesting that none of the above information was thought worthy of a headline.

You magazine saw it slightly differently. In the 4 June 2009 edition, this was their take on the matter:

> In March he [van der Westhuizen] was appointed chief executive at Progressive Investment Holdings (PIH). When

the company was placed under curatorship and a newspaper implicated Joost in irregularities, he not only lost his salary but also his sponsorship from the luxury Nondela Drakensberg Mountain Estate, from which he apparently received R50 000 a month.

The fact that all their facts were wrong didn't get in the way of this juicy little bit of proof that Joost was obviously tainted when it came to matters financial.

In the first sentence, they get his starting month wrong. They get his job appointment wrong. Which unnamed newspaper implicated Joost in financial irregularities? How did he lose a salary from a company from which he had resigned? '*Despite the incorrect facts, dear reader, please believe us when we now tell you that he lost a sponsorship worth R50 000 a month. How do we know? As usual when it comes to Joost van der Westhuizen, our sources are impeccable*' (my italics).

Another instance where the media chose to twist the facts to serve their own purposes was when, in 1997, Joost was sponsored by Abel du Toit (Toitjie) through his Nissan agency. For the next six years Joost was given the use of a sponsored Nissan vehicle. In 2006, Toitjie started a luxury development at Zilkaats Nek between Brits and Hartebeespoort Dam, and he asked the Van der Westhuizens, as a family, to promote the development for a fee. Joost happily agreed – he had by then dealt with Toitjie for a number of years without any problems.

Joost was not involved in the actual development of the property – Toitjie simply paid him to be its 'face'. Then, in 2008, Toitjie was sequestrated, mainly because of the poor performance of his motor franchises. Although the Zilkaats Nek project was fundamentally sound, it was part of Toitjie's personal estate and thus formed part of the assets that were liquidated. The Van der Westhuizens' contract had ended in 2006, but in 2009 Joost was blamed by the press for the failure of the development.

The 30 May–5 June 2009 edition of *heat* magazine declared: 'The Van der Westhuizens' Zilkaats Estate near Hartebeespoort is going bust. The knock to Joost's credibility has no doubt affected other income streams …'

On 4 June 2009, *You* magazine reported: 'The luxurious Zilkaats Estate near Hartebeesport Dam went into liquidation after Joost and his family were appointed ambassadors *three years ago* (my italics) …' Never let the facts get in the way of a good story.

Joost's role in the development consisted of appearing with his family in the official sales brochure. On an inside page of the brochure it says:

1995 Rugby World Cup star Joost van der Westhuizen endorses the development, saying: 'Zilkaats is a dynamic environment with the perfect balance of nature and activities to raise a successful family in. It is the kind of place that reminds you that a home is more than a building and location is more than a site, and at the end of the day the things you surround yourself with are the things that bring more to life. Zilkaats gives your family the privacy and space to explore, but also gives you peace of mind with the knowledge that they are in a safe and secure environment. Buying at Zilkaats doesn't just mean buying a home, it means creating a lifestyle … a great lifestyle.'

It is inconceivable from the above that anyone could be under the impression that Joost was the developer. On the back of the last page of the extravagant brochure, the logo and telephone number of the Pam Golding estate agency appear. To anyone looking for a property, the fact that a reputable agency had been appointed to conduct the sales would surely have been an infinitely more creditable endorsement of the project than the above anodyne sales spiel delivered by Joost.

It also would have taken any reporter worth their salt only minutes to discover who the actual developer was. But it was far easier to go for the headlines with the name Joost van der Westhuizen.

30

Writing Joost's book VII

My life seems to be ruled by my cellphone – whose isn't? Actually, to be precise, by text messages. The other night, while taking a rare break from my new life of 'Joost Doing It' by having a beer in my favourite restaurant, Giles, I received a text message from my NBF. It was very late, but I had been expecting a message to confirm our next meeting, so I wasn't too concerned when my phone beeped. (Also, I had copied Joost in on the first chapters of the manuscript I had emailed to the publishers that afternoon. I was thus expecting a few critical comments.) His message read: 'I want to say "fuck you", Gemmell, but not yet. I am tired and lying in bed reading our book. Problem is, I can't put it down. Stuff you! I need some sleep.'

As I read the first few words, I must confess that a cold shiver ran down my spine; but as I started getting the point of his message, I relaxed and smiled. I realised that his sense of humour was becoming more understated; more English than Afrikaans? I attributed this to his spending so much time in close proximity to an 'Engelsman'. (On the basis of my theory, might something inadvertently rub off on me? Might I already be a better scrumhalf?)

Then, at 3.38 a.m. on the Sunday morning, my phone beeped and flashed ominously to announce the arrival of a new message. There is no news so fantastic that it needs to be sent at that time of the morning. It was thus with deep foreboding that I scrabbled anxiously for my reading glasses in the blinking light of my cellphone. The message was from Joost's manager, Jenny. It read: 'Joost has collapsed and is in Sunninghill Hospital ... Will call as soon as I know more – J.'

Oh god! Now what? My mind went into overdrive, wondering what the hell had happened, while at the same time every fibre of my being craved another message to let me know that everything was going to be okay.

The longed-for message arrived about an hour later, in the form of a call from a tired-sounding Jenny. From what she could gather from talking to Amor at the hospital, Joost had returned from rugby some time around 8 p.m. and claimed to have had just three beers. (Apparently Amor had asked him how much he had had to drink when he walked in – as wives do.) The reason he hadn't drunk much, he explained, was because he had people coming to their house for a meeting, for which he wanted to be clear-headed.

It was during that meeting that Joost suddenly clutched his chest, pitched forward out of his chair and fell to the floor, where he lay comatose. Fortunately, one of the people present immediately started administering CPR while Amor called the paramedics.

By the time Jenny arrived at Sunninghill Hospital in the wee hours of the morning, Joost was in intensive care, attached to a number of exotic machines and heavily sedated. This, she was told, was just a precaution, as they didn't want the patient to wake up and start thrashing about, which apparently sometimes happened. The duty staff assured Jenny that Joost was going to be all right.

Later in the morning, Jenny called again to give me a blow-by-blow account. The story was mainly the same, although Jenny was now able to fill in a few details. She mentioned that Joost's family were all with him. Interestingly, one of the first people to have arrived at his bedside after his admittance to hospital had been Gustav, Joost's estranged brother.

A day later, when I was finally allowed to visit my almost-ex-subject, I discovered a remarkably docile Joost lying in bed with tubes up his nose and dozens of little electrode-patch-thingies stuck all over him. He smiled wanly and said, 'Thanks for the message,' referring to a text I'd sent him when I'd heard that he wasn't in imminent danger of shuffling off his mortal coil. It read: 'Sorry to hear about your collapse; you ex-rugby players aren't as tough as you look. Seems you'll do anything to get out of work ... Gemmell.'

Amor was there. 'Have you seen the papers?' she asked, thrusting a bundle at me. I hadn't.

I didn't stay long, as Joost looked very tired and his eyes kept closing. I took the newspapers and retired to a little lounge just off the ICU ward, where Amor and Jenny had set up base.

The papers were astonishing. They could have been reporting on a completely different incident. Not one article was factually correct. The worst was Rapport's *front-page story. It made a number of wild, woolly and completely outlandish statements, most of which were attributed to former bouncer Mike Bolhuis, Joost's sometime spokesperson, bodyguard and undoubtedly worst decision – ever.*

The papers also, without exception, found some way of linking Joost's collapse to the infamous video.

Amor joined me and ran through the various articles, highlighting the absurdities, suppositions and blatant falsehoods they all contained. 'See what we have to deal with?' she snapped. 'It happens all the bloody time. If they don't know the facts, they make them up. And Bolhuis – who does he think he is?'

She grabbed her cellphone from the coffee table in front of her and made a call.

'Listen, Mike,' she said, 'what do you think you're playing at? We asked you a dozen times NOT to talk to the press. But the papers are full of Mike Bolhuis said this and Mike Bolhuis said that. You weren't even there!'

A heated conversation ensued, which ended abruptly when Amor unequivocally stated that Bolhuis was fired; he was to say nothing to any publication; he was not to pretend he represented the family to anyone; and he was to 'Once and for all, SHUT UP!'

As Amor switched off the phone, she held out her left hand. 'Look!' she said. It was shaking. You have to be tough to make that sort of phone call. I decided then and there that, if for whatever reason I ever had to fight the Van der Westhuizens, I would start with Joost.

Compared to the gorgeous, fiery, pocket dynamo sitting next to me, he would be a pushover ...

The next day, when I visited him, Joost showed me a get-well card he'd received from some British & Irish Lions supporters. It came with a huge bunch of flowers and a red British & Irish Lions supporter's cap.

> *What do you get a Springbok who has achieved so much? The obvious answer is pretty flowers and a B&I Lions' cap (lovingly signed by two Brits). Being serious, you are an inspiration to many and it's a pleasure knowing you (albeit for a short time).*
>
> *Be strong and get well very soon.*
>
> *All our love & best wishes – Richard and Elisa.*

'At least it didn't get lost in all the flowers and cards that haven't been sent by the Springboks and their supporters,' Joost observed drily. Then he laughed. 'I think I would have to die first before they send anything. Look at Michael Jackson ... most of those people mourning him were the very ones condemning him for his weird behaviour when he was alive. Death seems to have wiped the slate clean for him. I cocked up – again! I didn't have the sense to die.'

'Well, you still might,' I said to cheer him up. But as he would be discharged in the next day or two, he probably wasn't likely to suddenly expire – I was giving him false hope.

Mind you, it would be better if he didn't pop off, as I needed him to finish the book!

31

Collapse

The Springbok Rugby Legends organisation appointed Joost to be a celebrity host in the Virgin Atlantic box at Loftus Versfeld for the second test against the British & Irish Lions on 27 June 2009. Joost mentions that he had noticed from the Wednesday prior to the test how he had continually felt tired and was very short-tempered with everyone, including, most unusually, his children.

He also claims not to have been sleeping properly the previous couple of months. Being grumpy and short-tempered, he wasn't really looking forward to hosting a bunch of Englishmen. But, as it turned out, he found the Poms surprisingly good company.

Because he was on duty, he practised his old habit of opening his own beers and keeping the tops in his pocket so that he could tell how many he had drunk at a moment's notice. 'Despite being in the suite virtually the whole day,' he says, 'when I left Loftus I had three bottle tops in my pocket. I knew I had a meeting at home, and because I was actually working – and I suppose because I wasn't feeling particularly great – I had carefully paced myself.'

He recalls that while he was in the Virgin box at Loftus, John Allan and Gavin Verejes from the Legends popped in to see him. 'Because their organisation had appointed me to host the Virgin people, they were just checking on how things were going. I remember Gavin saying to me, "Why are you so irritable?" Anyway, when I got home, I had my meeting. At the end of it I stood up to see the people off. The next memory I have is of waking up in a bed somewhere, demanding that a nurse take the tubes out of my throat. Amor was there, saying to me, "Don't worry, you can breathe … you can breathe …"

'It was horrible when they took the pipes out – they ran right into my lungs. But it seems I then fell asleep, so the next time I knew what was going on, it was Monday morning.'

Amor fills in some of the gaps. 'He came home grumpy, but he had already been angry when I called him before he got back. When I asked him what was wrong, he just said he was tired. He didn't look good when he arrived home. He looked half-asleep and was very pale. His 1 000-mile stare was more like a 2 000-mile stare,' she laughs. 'He was also pulling on his left shoulder while he was sitting chatting. Actually, he was listening more than talking. I secretly thought he was just looking for sympathy. I remember thinking he had had a great time at the rugby, but I had had the kids all day and was also quite tired.'

When one of their guests stood up and said goodbye and Joost didn't appear to hear her, Amor knew something definitely wasn't right. 'With that Joost pulled up backwards and fell on the floor, hitting his head on the tiles. Our guests put a pillow under his head and said it looked as if he was sleeping. But I immediately thought 'paramedics' – I was panicking but outwardly calm. Because of an incident in which Jordan got burnt about a year ago, we had the paramedics' number on a fridge magnet. I dialled the number and got through in seconds. I told them my husband had passed out and to please send someone. You can't believe it. They got here in about three minutes.'

In the meantime, Joost had stopped breathing, but fortunately one of the guests started administering CPR. With that, the paramedics walked in. Joost suddenly started shaking 'like he was having a seizure', says Amor. 'His head was jerking up and down – it was like a fit.'

Amor called Joost's parents and brother Pieter, who all agreed to come through. 'I went with Joost in the ambulance and we raced off to Sunninghill Hospital. They were waiting for him when he got there. I was amazed at the level of efficiency. You always hear about problems, but the way they handled us was just fantastic.'

Amor was put in a waiting room while Joost was taken for various scans and checks.

'One moment I was almost getting ready to go to bed, just as soon as our guests left, and the next I was sitting in the ER section of a hospital. I wondered, "What the hell happened?" It was weird. The kids' faces kept popping into my head. I couldn't stop myself thinking, "They need a father; he has to be okay for them. They can't live without him." It was awful.'

It didn't get any better when she was allowed in to see Joost. He was connected to a life-support machine and had tubes running down his throat into his lungs. 'Obviously I had never seen him like that. It was hard to see. I remember just sitting next to him, holding his hand.'

Joost's parents arrived at about 1 p.m. in the morning, and his brothers arrived soon afterwards. Unfortunately for Amor, her parents were overseas. 'It's funny, but I felt so alone. It didn't matter that there were other people around, I just wanted my mom and dad to be there.'

Then, at some stage, the nurse wanted to remove the tubes to Joost's lungs so that he could breathe on his own. That appears to be when Joost woke up for the first time, as he remembers.

Says Amor: 'He was very angry and threatened to pull out the tubes if the nurse didn't remove them. Also, he couldn't remember anything and kept asking why he was there.'

Then she says, 'Strangely, the first thing he said to me was, "I saw my *oupa* Joost. He was walking towards me in a field and he shook my hand. He said I was okay."' At that point, Amor nearly went to pieces. 'It was all so weird.'

Amor only got to go home at about four o'clock in the afternoon. She was shattered. 'When I think about it, I was tired before the whole drama started. So by then I was *really* exhausted.'

She picked up her bag and her coat and, as she was walking out of the hospital, a woman walked up to her and said, 'Amor ...' and tried to hand her a bunch of flowers and a card.

'Something said to me, "Be careful,"' said Amor.

The woman with the flowers then said, 'I'm Yvonne Beyers from *Huisgenoot*. We're so sorry to hear about Joost, but can we do an interview with you?'

'I said to her, "How dare you? How dare you? How dare you have the audacity to stand in front of me and ask me that question? Let me ask *you* a question. Are you happy with what you have achieved? Are you happy my husband is in intensive care? Fuck you!"'

And she stalked off.

Amor walked into her house to find Pieter reading the *Rapport* newspaper, which was carrying a story on the girl from the infamous video. 'On the front page was a picture of her. She had her legs open, wearing a Springbok jersey with a 9 on it. I just started laughing. At that point it was all too much. I think she was having a direct go at me, because I had at times gone on stage wearing Joost's No. 9 jersey.'

The children's reaction to their father's collapse was interesting. When Amor told Jordan that Joost had fallen and hit his head and had had to go to hospital, he immediately asked if his dad had gone in an ambulance. When Amor said he had, Jordan asked, 'Were you scared, Mommy?'

'I thought it was remarkably intuitive for a five-year-old to ask a question like that,' Amor says proudly. 'Kylie was very quiet. While Jordan was asking all sorts of questions, she just ignored me. However, when I took them to the hospital, after the nurses had removed all Joost's tubes, Jordan became withdrawn and Kylie was full of beans. But they are fine now. Glad to have their daddy home.'

Joost says that Jordan keeps asking him if he is going away again. 'Kylie keeps on popping in to check that I'm still here,' he laughs.

While the whole drama was unfolding, Amor discovered that there was a flaw in the master of her new CD, which she was supposed to sign off because of its imminent release.

'Because of everything, I hadn't been able to fetch the master to listen to it in order to be able to approve it. Then, after they delivered the master to me, I listened to it on the way to the hospital and picked up a glitch on one of the tracks. But when I phoned my record company they said that they had already made the glass master.'

The glass master is an expensive piece of the process and Amor started to feel that the whole world was against her. 'Eventually I called Kosie, the CEO of the company, and he was fantastic. He told me not to worry, he would sort it out.

'But the worst part of everything was the press. The phones simply did not stop ringing. Also, I had Joost's cellphone and they were sending him messages! He was in ICU and there were text messages coming through, asking for a statement. There was a letter in the *Citizen* on the Tuesday that summed it all up. It said, "When will the press be happy? When he is dead? Or when the marriage is broken and they get divorced? When does it end?" It seems never,' she says, shaking her head.

Back home, Joost found he was very tired. 'I was speaking to my GP, Henry Kelbrick, and he said that it wasn't serious if you only had one fit. But if you have another one, then there is a serious problem. So we will have to see. But the really irritating thing is the press started hounding Amor, Bridget (Joost's publicist) and me to ask why I'd had to have a toxic-screening blood test. We never chose to have any tests done on me. The hospital decided what tests they had to do.'

The media were seemingly implying that Amor had wanted to check whether Joost had been taking drugs; conversely, they were insinuating that there was some kind of connection between having such a test and the video, in which, allegedly, drugs were snorted.

Joost said bitterly, 'On that Saturday, Barend van Graan, the CEO of the Blue Bulls, also collapsed after the rugby. But the press never asked him why he had undergone the exact same blood test. It's just amazing. Oh, and former Springbok flank Ruben Kruger collapsed while driving and he had the same tests; did anyone want to know why *he* had to have them?'

32

Writing Joost's book VIII

I am at Giles, talking to my friend, the garrulous Peter Wales, when one of his business associates joins us. I haven't met him before, but he seems vaguely familiar. It takes a while, but then it dawns on me – the reason I find him familiar is that he looks remarkably like Joost. With a slight change in hairstyle, a pair of jeans and a white shirt, and a scowl, he will be a dead ringer for my NBF.

'You know who you look like?' I ask.

'Joost van der Westhuizen,' he says without hesitation. 'I can't see it, but a lot of people have told me I look like him.'

'We could use you!' I get all excited. 'You can be the guy in the bloody video who is supposed to be Joost.'

He laughs. 'God, wouldn't that be a laugh!'

The more we drink, the more we think such a ruse would solve everything. 'All you need is one or two small facial scars and we would have to bugger up your little finger – then we could go visit heat *magazine and put the fear of death into those bastards. Hope your dick is bigger than Joost's ...' Funny how few beers it takes to become really sharp.*

I take the lookalike's business card. There has to be an angle. I'm not sure how, but I am sure he can be useful. I can't count the number of times I've heard from sanctimonious know-it-alls that if a look-alike Joost exists, we all will have known about him long ago. Really? I didn't know about Simon Storm, and he looks just like Joost. He is the same age and, coincidentally, when he played rugby in Durban, he played scrumhalf.

On my way home I call the long-suffering Jenny and tell her of my find. She isn't nearly as excited as I am and, curiously, seems more concerned about me getting home in one piece.

While having a beer with Joost and Amor and chatting about nothing in particular, she suddenly asks me, 'Has Joost told you about all his children?'

I can't believe it – more scandal! Is this good or bad? And I'd thought we had enough on our hands with the bloody video.

'No, tell me,' I say carefully.

'How many is it, babe – about 14?' Amor asks, looking at Joost from where she is reclining comfortably on a couch.

Fourteen! Gosh, the man is prolific! But of course I realise that we can't be talking about his *children. I can't imagine the gorgeous, albeit fiery, Amor being quite so relaxed were these children actually Joost's progeny ...*

'These are kids with cancer,' Amor explains. 'Joost has "adopted" them in the sense that he goes and visits them, and where possible does activities with them; he takes them on outings – that sort of stuff.'

Joost takes up the story, 'So far I've lost 14 of the kids I've been visiting ...'

'Gosh, maybe you'd better stop visiting?' I offer facetiously. He almost smiles.

'Until you have seen kids as sick as these, you will never know how tough life really can be. I remember one kid at the Unitas Hospital in Pretoria. He was about 13 years old and he told me that his family had a house near where we lived on the dam. So I said, "That's great. When you get out of here we'll go skiing and have a party on my boat." He looked up and said, "You know I'm not getting out of here ..." God, it broke my heart. Tragically, the day after I saw him, he died.'

Joost then tells the story of a nine-year-old Bulls fan. 'I was still playing rugby and apparently this little chap had said I was his hero and he would love to meet me. So I decided to go through and visit him on the Wednesday afternoon, which was my rest day. But on the Monday, John Williams, our coach, gave us the day off. So I decided to rather go and visit the child then. It was unbelievable; he was nine years old, but he was half the size Jordan is now, and he's five.'

When Joost walked into the ward, the boy recognised him and smiled. His parents just burst into tears; it was the first time in months their son had smiled. Joost gave the boy a signed cap and a Bulls jersey. He then sat with the extremely ill little tyke for a while. 'He was half-asleep, and I just stroked him as he lay on my lap. He had drips and tubes coming out of everywhere. It was unbelievably sad.'

The little boy was in Vereeniging, and after spending an hour with the frail little fellow, it took Joost about two hours to get back to Loftus Versfeld in Pretoria. As he parked at the stadium, Joost got a call from the hospital to say the boy had died.

'I believe he probably just let go,' says Amor. 'He had almost certainly been hanging on to see Joost, and then once he had achieved his dream, his body said, "Fine, I can go."'

33

Writing Joost's book IX

Around the time the video was released, I wrote the article below. Because I subsequently starting working on the book with Joost, I neither completed the article nor submitted it for publication. But reading it again recently, I felt the sentiments remained peculiarly apt.

The Girls Who Are after Joost van der Westhuizen

Who would want to be Joost van der Westhuizen? For years he played his heart out to become one of South Africa's greatest rugby players, only to be crash-tackled by the selfsame media that profitably promoted his wife's music and their ostensibly perfect showbiz marriage.

The minute the popular press discovered an incriminating video, supposedly of their favourite son, they thrust it into the public domain with amazing haste. Many questions have arisen out of this tacky affair, most of which have already been keenly debated. But one that still needs to be explained is: Who are the girls hounding Joost's marriage into a premature grave – and why?

Melinda Shaw is the editor of *heat* magazine, the gossip rag that broke the video story. This is what she said about Amor before she decided to print the story: 'When we saw the video for the first time, we were just as shocked as you are now. We cringed on behalf of Joost and immediately thought of Amor.' So what route did her thoughts take?

Did she think, 'Here we have a video, made with the intent of bringing a man down – ruining his marriage, his family, his reputation, his life and more – but made by people who obviously have society's best interests at heart'? (After all, the note to *heat* magazine did say, 'We decided to make the video because Joost was our role model and he just can't do all that stuff. We also didn't do it for money.') Did she 'think' she should support such civic-minded people?

Or did she think, 'I have to break this story, because it will help Amor realise what Joost is really like. Granted, it will ruin the lovely family life her kids enjoy, but it will show that, apart from being a fantastic father, a reliable breadwinner and one of South Africa's sporting greats, Joost is a drug-taking cheat. And that, of course, is much more important for everyone to know'?

So she ran the story. In the process, she philanthropically paid some cash to the decent citizens who had made the video. (The same ones who said that they didn't do it for the money.) She also jolly decently agreed to respect their confidentiality.

And the civilised producers of the video, who were so upset with Joost for doing 'all that stuff'? So upset that they enticed a stripper to secretly film a liaison, approved her use of drugs (they don't appear to have shopped her ...) and, eight months later (*subsequently proved to be incorrect*), 'gave' the video to a gossip magazine? Obviously, such behaviour is of a higher moral standard than 'all that stuff'. It deserves payment and confidentiality.

Shaw's explanations as to why she launched the media onslaught on the hapless Joost and Amor reminded me of the people who used to try to defend apartheid. How do you defend the indefensible?

Melinda Shaw does not have children. In fact, Melinda Shaw doesn't have a husband – although she certainly seems to know a thing or two about ensuring that other people don't keep theirs.

Then there's Esmaré Weideman, editor of *You* magazine. In one of her editorials, she calls radio personality Martin Gillingham 'a motor-mouthed little deejay down in Cape Town who has so few brain cells he makes his living from slagging off whichever name he manages to spell each morning'.

Please note that this polite little gem comes from someone who makes a living out of revealing people's deepest, darkest secrets. It appears that not long ago Weideman was very cross with Steve Hofmeyr. Apparently he was having an affair and has children by four different women. Steve, in turn, got angry with Esmaré, believing her to be partly responsible for breaking up his marriage. At the 2008 Miss South Africa pageant at Sun City, he threw a cup of (cold) tea in Esmaré's face. She is now suing him for abuse. Obviously being assailed by a cold liquid is, by her standards, far more scandalous a crime than helping to break up someone's marriage.

Lastly there is Liza Albrecht at *Rapport* newspaper. The adage 'People who live in glass houses shouldn't throw stones' springs to mind.

The way in which the girl in the video is now being fêted by the media is a curious phenomenon. She is being treated with enormous respect, as if she has somehow performed a valuable public duty in exposing a man's weaknesses by enticing him into a set-up in which drugs and hidden cameras played a role. Apparently she is now worthy of respect and adulation (she has been featured in FHM, *is the star of a photo shoot in* heat *magazine (2–8 May 2009), and is also featured in another edition, where she shows off her new breasts).*

Bearing in mind that she was assisted in her little flirtation with fame by none other than her then boyfriend, one wonders how he felt seeing his girlfriend grinding her naked breasts into some other man's groin. Did it turn him on?

Note to *heat* magazine (as published by them) from video-makers (my additions in italics)

'I am the person who supplied the video to *heat*. We decided to make the video because Joost was our role model and he just can't do all that stuff. We also didn't do it for money. *(So we decided to collude with drug-taking strippers in a clever bit of entrapment.)*

The reason we could do it was because Joost had seen the girl before for the same things. *(Not sure how we know this, because she isn't our type of girl.)* The fact that we also heard that Joost had cheated with other girls was also a big thing for us. *(We have never sinned and therefore have a right to be angry when other people do. Also, we had 'heard', which was good enough for us.)* She has no children.

The video was made about eight months ago. *(Wrong – it was made in 2006.)* It was made in a house in Moreleta Park. It was made late one afternoon. We got together and put the camera in a handbag. We had to cut it to hide it. We also piled clothes on top of it. *(We were so angry, we waited eight months before we gave the video to a magazine.)*

We waited this long before handing it in as we were waiting for enough time to pass. *(Which we found is what happens when you wait – time passes.)* And though many people think it's not Joost, it is Joost on the video! *(Because we say so.)* Mike Bolhuis also did not make any contact with any of us. *(Are they lying, Mike?)*

The girl also doesn't want to make contact with anybody. *(So her income has gone down? You can't believe how difficult it is to make a living as a stripper without making contact.)* And that is why there won't be any statement from her. I hope that this statement will solve much and that the truth will come out.' *(We are great believers in the truth, as long as it isn't about us or revealing who the stripper is.)*

Signed: The man who supplied the video. *(Obviously a man who stands for truth and fair play; for good marriages; for no cheating; for no drugs and for confidentiality.)*

34

Video (nearly)
killed the rugby star

In order to put the video into some kind of perspective, it might be apposite to quote from an article by award-winning journalist Beauregard Tromp, which appeared in the *Star* at the height of the feeding frenzy surrounding the infamous tape:

> Lots of talking, a bit of sniffing but very little action …
>
> He makes a half-hearted attempt to grope her. She makes a go at oral sex. And just as things seem to be getting under way, the CD gets stuck. 'Joost' quickly jumps up to fix it and quickly returns to the action. Only moments later, the music interrupts a second time.
>
> Ultimately there's no standing ovation as 'Joost' fails to respond 'manfully' to the incentives …
>
> This seems to encourage the girl, now clad only in a G-string, to continue her monologue about her mother, her aunt and her boyfriend, who 'doesn't do these kinds of things. At all.'
>
> Throughout the frustrating 29-minute video, the girl uses every opportunity to fiddle with the camera inside her bag …

Hardly sounds like it would give *Deep Throat*, the iconic porn film made in the 1970s, a run for its money.

The fascinating aspect of the whole sordid affair is how much editorial such a dull, incredibly un-salacious and, for all its pretensions, completely sexless 29-minute film has generated.

Based on the hysterical reaction to the whole scandal, it becomes fascinating to contemplate what the public's reaction would have been had one of South Africa's favourite sons participated in an orgy with paid prostitutes similar to the one in which Max Mosley, president of the FIA (Fédération Internationale de l'Automobile), was filmed enjoying himself.

Mosley, 68, the son of the 1930s British fascist leader Sir Oswald Mosley, sued the Sunday tabloid paper *News of the World* for grossly invading his privacy after it printed pictures and published a video of him indulging in a five-hour sadomasochistic sex session with prostitutes in a Chelsea apartment.

He simply declared that what he did in his private capacity was not anyone's business except his wife's and took the offending publication to court, where he won £60 000 in damages (the highest award in recent legal history in a privacy action). That should keep him in orgies for a number of years to come. He was also awarded costs.

On Saturday 14 February 2009, Amor was preparing for a show at the Marula Sun and Joost was getting ready to commentate on a Super 14 game (Bulls versus Reds) at Loftus, when he received a call from Gavin Prins, a journalist with *Rapport*. Apparently the paper was in possession of a videotape allegedly showing Joost frolicking with a girl in a pink thong and snorting an unidentified white powder. Prins wanted Joost to comment on the tape, as the paper intended to announce the existence of the video in their next day's edition.

Joost asked how he could comment on something he hadn't seen (perhaps not the best response), and Gavin said he would call back. Joost immediately phoned a friend who happened to be a lawyer, Johann Steyn, who wanted to know if he should try to get an interdict. For this to happen, Joost would have had to cancel his commentary job to attend court, which he didn't want to do.

'It was my work – I couldn't cancel at such short notice, and also I didn't know what it was about and what or who we would be interdicting.'

Prins called back and asked if Joost was going to get an interdict. 'No, I'm not – go ahead and write what you want,' said Joost.

He then immediately informed Amor about Prins's call. Later, while Amor was on her way to the Marula Sun, Esmaré Weideman of *Huisgenoot* phoned her and said, 'I hope you are sitting down.' She then repeated the story about the video and wanted to know what Amor was going to do. Amor declined to chat.

After the rugby, Joost joined Amor at her function. 'Obviously it bothered us the whole night,' says Joost. While they were still at the Marula Sun, Amor received a text message from Marcus Brewster, a publicist, who offered to do damage control. Joost phoned Brewster and asked him how he knew about the video.

Brewster said that somebody in the media had called him around 11 a.m. that morning to ask how a celebrity was likely to react if accused of appearing in such a video. 'The whole thing was very strange – suddenly everyone knew about this video,' says Joost angrily. He did, however, reluctantly engage Brewster to assist in dealing with the media. Brewster immediately appointed a chap called Hein Kaiser to deal with the matter.

The arrangement lasted hardly a week before Joost discovered that Brewster was connected to the Media24 group – the same group that housed *heat* magazine and *Huisgenoot*. Joost terminated Kaiser's services, but subsequently received a bill from Marcus Brewster for R62 000, which, to date, he has refused to pay.

The next morning, on Sunday 15 February 2009, *Rapport* hit the streets with a front-page headline that read:

Joost in seks-video
(Joost in sex-video)
Skokbeelde van kaal Bok wat poeier snuif
(Shock images of naked Bok sniffing powder)

'It was a horrible, horrible day,' says Joost. 'I can't describe how awful it all was. I tried to get hold of the paper's lawyers to see if I could watch [the video], but because it was Sunday, we couldn't get anything arranged.'

On the Monday, Joost went to the offices of the legal firm Werksmans, which represents Media24, to watch the video in which he was accused of having a starring role. He watched about 15 minutes of it, then left.

In the meantime, one of his former-policeman friends (someone who apparently sails close to the wind and whom Joost would rather not name) had referred him to 'top' lawyers who were going to help him with the debacle. When Joost met with them, he unaccountably felt very uncomfortable with his new 'saviours'. They wanted to know whether Joost had any identifying features on his body or whether he had evidence that could prove it wasn't him in the video. 'I don't know any of you,' said Joost, 'so for the time being I'll keep my evidence to myself. Shouldn't we be investigating the wrongs and rights of this matter rather than investigating me?'

They chatted for a while, and then one of the lawyers suggested that they go and watch the video. Joost said he didn't need to watch the video again, and made the remark that would backfire on him forever more. 'Apart from anything,' he said, 'that guy's dick is bigger than mine.' And he started to laugh. It was a throwaway line; a joke. (Much later, some wag on a blog said, 'He should have said the guy's dick was SMALLER. Who would have known …?')

The next morning, Joost read his 'joke' in the papers. A remark made in the supposed confidentiality of attorneys' offices had found its way into the media. It is not surprising that Joost feels paranoid about everyone he interacts with and why he so often resorts to working with people he has dealt with in the past, regardless of how unconventional their methods or unlikely their occupations. This is also how he ended up with Mike Bolhuis as his spokesman. Mike Bolhuis is a former bouncer turned private investigator. He has apparently been involved in cleaning up the notoriously corrupt bouncer industry.

While Joost was married to Marlene, the Van der Westhuizens lived a couple of kilometres from Bolhuis and came to know him reasonably well. When Mike phoned and offered to help, it seemed like a godsend. According to Joost, 'At least he was neither a policeman nor a lawyer.'

But at that point, 'Team van der Westhuizen' (Joost's manager Jenny was not in the country at this time), as they collectively became labelled by *heat* magazine, started making silly statements. Far from exonerating the beleaguered Joost, they had the opposite effect of further implicating him.

Bolhuis claimed to have found the girl in the video. He said that he had interviewed her and that she had made a statement that the person in the video wasn't Joost. There was just one problem with his account – the real girl emerged and said that she had never met or spoken to Mike Bolhuis. (In an increasingly tangled web of statements, she apparently later recanted and said she *had* met Bolhuis.)

Joost also did his bit to assist Bolhuis in making a mockery of Team van der Westhuizen's defence. His own inane remarks – that he did not own Polo socks or have 'holey' underwear, and claiming that his maid was under instruction to throw out old clothes with holes in them – did not help his cause.

One could probably interpret the silly comments in a number of ways. They were either the desperate attempts of an innocent man to show that the video was fake and he had nothing to do with it, or, conversely, they were the statements of a drowning man looking for anything to keep him afloat.

Bolhuis also claimed to have found the people who had made the video – two brothers, one a former policeman and one who was still in the police force. The problem with Bolhuis's claim this time was that *heat* magazine and *Rapport* had found the person who actually *had* made the video (or so he claims ...).

They published his handwritten statement, in which he says: *'Mike Bolhuis het ook geen kontak met niemand van ons gemaak nie'* – Mike Bolhuis also made no contact with any one of us. He omitted to explain who the 'us' was. Bolhuis also couldn't or wouldn't produce the statements he had promised.

In the interim, Joost received a bill for R101 073.61 from Van Der Linde Attorneys, who had been handling the matter. These were the same lawyers from whose offices the 'smaller dick' comment had migrated to the press. Interestingly, after the bill was sent to be assessed by the Law Society, Theresa van der Linde suddenly reduced it to R80 000 – an amount Joost paid reluctantly.

'For nothing,' he says. 'I can't think of a single thing they actually did for me. I stopped using them when they told me they couldn't represent me if I used Mike Bolhuis. Well, they did nothing except run up bills. So I went to Mike.'

The *heat* magazine edition of 30 May 2009 had a slightly different angle regarding the lawyer's bill. Their story reads:

> It is understood that Van der Linde, who represented Team van der Westhuizen for only six days before resigning the case, charged Joost less than R100 000. According to the LSSA (Law Society of South Africa), that's well within the average. And these fees wouldn't have come as a surprise to Joost ... 'The lawyer and client would agree on a rate before any work begins. The rates are all very different and vary from one lawyer to the next,' says Thinus Grobler, director of the LSSA.

In anybody's book, R100 000 (it was actually more, not less as *heat* magazine stated) is a large amount of money for just six days' work. It means that Theresa van der Linde, who represented Joost, was paid approximately R16 000 a day while she was on the case, or somewhere around R2 000 an hour. While R2 000 per hour is apparently not an unreasonable rate for a senior attorney (according to Joost, Theresa was a junior), it is quite impressive that Van der Linde spent eight hours a day for six successive days working on Joost's case.

Presumably she was able to produce some evidence of all the work she had done, either in the form of written opinions, writs issued or sage advice dispensed to her client. If she did perform any of the aforementioned tasks, it is regrettable that she forgot to apprise Team van der Westhuizen of the fruits of her labours.

You magazine had the following to say in their 4 June 2009 edition:

> Joost recently objected to a R100 000 bill from the lawyer who briefly represented him in connection with the video scandal. He said it was excessive and although legal experts don't necessarily agree, Theresa van der Linde lowered her fee to R80 000.

You magazine omitted to mention that Theresa had been induced to reduce the bill to R80 000 only after Joost had threatened to have it assessed by the Law Society (to which the bill had already been sent) and that the reduction was not an act of largesse on her part.

An issue that is regularly raised in connection with the video saga is the fact that Joost hasn't sued any of the magazines or news-papers that have been taking potshots at him. Valid argument or not, it still takes a brave man – and a wealthy one at that – to sue the media. Van der Linde's bill was R101 073.61 for six days' work. What would lawyers' bills run to for a case that took months, or even years, to complete – with no guarantee of winning?

Joost is no doubt mindful of the fact that when Amor sued *Loslyf* magazine and its editor Eugene Goddard (she was claim-ing R1 million) for publishing a doctored photograph of her and was awarded R180 000, plus costs against Goddard, she never saw a cent from the former editor. (*Loslyf* settled out of court.) Goddard had sequestrated himself just before judgment was handed down and to date none of the awarded costs have been recovered.

Consequently, first-hand experience of the perils of litigating hardly filled the Van der Westhuizens with optimism.

When the options available to Joost van der Westhuizen under South African law are considered, they actually present a rather bleak choice. Suing for defamation has the effect of exacerbating the case and keeping the story alive. This is always a quandary for would-be plaintiffs – do they sue with the risks attendant to this sort of litigation and highlight the defamation for months, if not years to come, or do they lie low and hope the matter blows over and is forgotten? What to do?

In their defence, the magazines will say that they published the story because it is in the public interest. Joost and Amor have been public figures for so long that the media can readily claim that how they conduct their lives is of interest to the man in the street. And for a legal suit to succeed, Joost would have to prove that it isn't him in the video and that the media knew this when they published the story.

But it can be difficult proving you are NOT someone. In fact, proving the negative of anything has always been problematic. Well-known Johannesburg attorney Richard Behrmann tells the story of a client maintaining, 'I never promised him a share and I have a witness to that effect.' Really?

Kelsey Stuart's *The Newspaperman's Guide to the Law* states that a public figure is defined as 'a person who, by his accomplishments, fame or mode of living, or by adopting a profession or calling that gives the public a legitimate interest in his doings, his affairs and his character, has become a "public person".' By that definition, Joost and Amor are, without doubt, 'public persons'.

Similarly the conclusion drawn by lawyer DJ McQuoid-Mason in his book *The Law of Privacy in South Africa* is that such a person is considered 'to a certain extent to have forfeited his right to privacy'.

But is that true? If you are a 'public figure', do you necessarily forfeit your right to privacy?

Taken to their logical conclusion, these hypotheses would mean that everything from bathing behaviour to the toilet habits (and of course sexual relations) of 'public persons' would be open season for publications wanting to print pictures or descriptions of same. However, in the USA, the *First Amendment Handbook of the Reporters' Committee for Freedom of the Press* states:

> Publication of truthful information concerning the private life of a person that would be both highly offensive to a reasonable person and not of legitimate public concern is an invasion of privacy. Liability often is determined by how the information was obtained, and its newsworthiness. Revealing private, sensational facts about a person's sexual activity, health or economic status can constitute an invasion of privacy.

Only problem for Joost is he lives in South Africa.

But what about Section 14 of our Constitution, which makes it quite clear that South Africans have the right to privacy?

**Section 14 of the Constitution of the
Republic of South Africa, Act 108 of 1996:**

14. Privacy:

a) Everyone has the right to privacy, which *includes* [my italics] the right not to have -
b) their person or home searched;
c) their property searched;
d) their possessions seized; or
e) the privacy of their communications infringed

Jane Duncan, the former executive director of the Freedom of Expression Institute, lectured at a seminar hosted by the South African Human Rights Commission on 23 October 2007. Her address was titled 'Privacy, Freedom of Expression and the Public Interest'. Some extracts from her speaking notes make interesting reading:

> What are justifiable limitations on the right to privacy? ... An invasion of privacy may include the acquisition and disclosure of private information by third parties, which is a violation of informational privacy rights. In terms of the right to privacy, people have a right to limit access to and dissemination of private information to others ... There is no magic formula when it comes to weighing up which comes first: the right to privacy or the public interest. Often, it may be in the public interest for private facts to remain precisely that: private ... Getting the balance right depends on the facts of a particular story, and involves high levels of judgement on the part of the media.

One can infer from the last comment that the role a magazine or newspaper plays in publishing stories in the public interest may be corrupted by its commercial motives. So, far from representing the public interest, magazines such as *heat*, *You* and *Huisgenoot*, and a newspaper such as *Rapport* (the main publishers pursuing the video scandal), can claim to represent nothing more than the interests of their shareholders.

A key question that should be asked is: Whose interests are really being served by the media in South Africa when they behave in such an intrusive and invasive manner?

If it is not financial consideration that dictates the media's actions, can they honestly say that they thought 'Joostgate' (as they so originally christened the scandal) was in the public interest and that is why they published the story? Did the fact that they might ruin a marriage in the process and the future of two young children not outweigh their noble, big-hearted concern for the public at large? Or was their object simply money after all? (Joost's cynical view is that when someone says 'It's not about the money; it's the principle ...', it is about the money ...)

Is it not a simple fact that whenever a newspaper or magazine features Joost or Amor, they practically guarantee doubling their circulation and, hence, their revenue? In reality, does the issue of ethics versus revenue ever arise at editorial meetings?

The dilemma caused by the muddy situation in South African law as to what constitutes invasion of privacy doesn't only affect so-called 'celebrities'. In 2008, when Kgalema Motlanthe was still president of the Republic of South Africa, the media ran a number of stories about his private life. Headlines mentioned that Motlanthe, a married man, was 'lonely' and having 'affairs'.

'When a politician is involved, entitlement to privacy melts away,' says publisher and editor Raymond Louw. This doesn't, however, appear to be the view of the majority of commentators.

Predictably, Motlanthe insisted that his private life was his own affair. Not so predictable was the support he received from the opposition party the Democratic Alliance, whose spokesman at the time, Paul Boughey, expressed the party view, saying: 'A person's private life should be respected.' Surprisingly, party leader – and former journalist – Helen Zille went along with it.

Presumably most South Africans would not appreciate having their private lives splashed all over the media in order to titillate and delight the masses. How hypocritical, then, when this privilege is not afforded to people who, by dint of their talents and industry, have brought untold pleasure to millions.

The paradox is that 'public persons' who have achieved, are successful and have enhanced others' lives are targeted for the dubious purpose of enriching a defined few (the media/their shareholders) who haven't excelled and so aren't themselves targets.

UNIVERSAL DECLARATION OF HUMAN RIGHTS

On 10 December 1948, the General Assembly of the United Nations adopted and proclaimed the Universal Declaration of Human Rights.

Article 12

No one shall be subjected to arbitrary interference with his *privacy* [my italics], family, home or correspondence, nor to attacks upon his honour and reputation. Everyone has the right to the protection of the law against such interference or attacks.

NB: This chapter is not supposed to be a definitive legal argument – it is merely the author's ramblings. As attorney Richard Behrmann, when checking this section, so kindly pointed out, 'Given that you aren't writing a legal textbook, and people won't exactly be looking to you for advice, this is fine ...'

35

Writing Joost's book X

One Sunday over lunch I have a discussion with a good friend of mine who is a talk-show host on a popular radio station. He is generally regarded as being one of the most powerful men in South African radio. He asks how the book is going, and then adds: 'Dave, be careful that you are not being used. Beware that you are not providing a cloak of respectability for Joost so that he can get out of this video thing.'

'Well,' I venture, 'it still hasn't been conclusively proven that it is him in the video.'

'Wake up, Dave,' my friend says. 'Of course it's him. Let me ask you something: What would you do – and you are not even a public figure – if someone published details of a video of someone purporting to be you, messing around with a girl and snorting drugs? What would you do without even thinking about it twice?'

'I'd sue them.'

'Precisely! Why isn't Joost suing the pants off them? Because it is him. Be careful. By all means, go ahead with the book; but make sure you write the real story and not just what they want you to write.'

I go on the internet and have another look at the edited extracts of the video on the heat magazine website. By now I have grown quite fond of Joost: his forthright way of dealing with things; his ability to take anything derogatory I throw at him regarding his conservative Afrikaans background; his doting and all-consuming delight in his kids; and his unflagging cheerfulness at seeing me.

As I watch the sordid little cameos on the screen, my heart tells me that the man I am watching is someone who only resembles Joost. But my head says, 'Sorry, without a shadow of a doubt, it's him.'

The next time I see Joost, I ask him how his investigations into the makers of the video are going.

'We're making progress,' he says. 'Quite soon I should be able to get a signed statement from the guy who made the tape.'

'Sorry, Joost,' I say. 'All the signed statements in the world will mean nothing. The only way you are going to settle this thing is to produce the guy in the video.'

'Oh, don't worry. We will,' Joost says.

But things have changed. I know that it is him in the video. Now what? Oh God.

I suddenly become obsessed with finding a Solomonesque solution. (When two women both claimed to be the mother of a baby they had brought before King Solomon, the wise king suggested that the child be cut in half and shared between the women. The real mother immediately said that she would rather see her child go to the other woman than have it killed.) At times my head spins as I juggle the options, none of which are any sort of option.

I lie in bed one morning wondering how I am going to honourably extricate myself from the project and where I can run away to, when it suddenly dawns on me that I should have done more research on the video. I have neither read all the articles on the video nor watched all the excerpts. Like Joost, I have simply hoped it would go away.

But it isn't going to go away, and Joost is not going to be able to produce a double. This means that I have to do something before the book project turns into a disaster.

I won't explain the mechanics, but I manage to contact the girl who appeared in the video. At first she is hesitant to meet with me, but after I explain that I will not publish a word without her approval and that I want to establish for myself who the guy in the video is from the 'horse's mouth', she agrees to see me.

We arrange to meet at a restaurant in Pretoria, and she texts me the address. Throughout the journey to meet her, my heart and brain engage each other in a tense conversation that goes something like this:

Heart: *She's a stripper. She doesn't know who Joost is — she was told that the guy they were setting up was Joost, and that's why she says it is him.*

Brain: *Yeah, right. How can a Pretoria chick not know who Joost is?*

Heart: *She's a stripper — what can she possibly know about rugby?*

Brain: *Okay. But where is the lookalike then? Are you trying to tell me that there is someone walking around these parts who looks exactly like Joost and no one has noticed him before now?*

Heart: *I'm sure when you think about it, there is probably a Joost lookalike in every little Afrikaner community in South Africa — he has very typical Afrikaner features.*

Brain: *Yeah, right ...*

I make my way through Pretoria and arrive at the restaurant, which is diagonally across from Loftus Versfeld. 'Oh dear,' says my heart, 'I think the stripper could be a rugby fan ...'

She is. But not a Blue Bulls fan — 'Ek hou van die Sharks,' she says, laughing.

After slightly self-conscious introductions, she introduces me to her friend Mariana, who is closer to my age and appears to have assumed the role of guardian to the girl. After discussing the information I want and confirming that I have no intention of either harming or endangering the girl, it is agreed that she will talk to me and that I can record the conversation.

Marlize is attractive. She has a slim figure with largish breasts, long blonde hair, unblemished skin, a ready, gap-toothed smile and long, elegant fingers. My head understands why Joost might have been attracted to her. My heart reluctantly agrees. She asks whether I mind if she talks in Afrikaans; she understands English but prefers to talk in her own language.

Unsurprisingly, Marlize van Emmenis's sordid but simple tale is far more plausible than Team van der Westhuizen's contention that the video is part of a huge Boeremafia plot.

The story centres on a jealous boyfriend who wanted to scare off a celebrity who was after his girlfriend. Marlize confirms that the video was made in 2006.

Apparently she first met Joost at a late-night drinking spot, where she gave him her phone number. When Joost subsequently sent her text messages late at night and also telephoned her, her boyfriend Anthony de Beer became irritated to the point where he hatched his grubby little revenge plot, with his girlfriend as bait.

Asked if she went along willingly or if she was coerced, Marlize replies, 'Anthony used to hit me and lock me in my room – I was very scared of him. So when he said that this was what we were going to do, I just had to go along with it.'

Why, I ask, did you not leave him if he hit you?

She responds simply: 'Because I loved him ...'

'What was he going to do with the video?'

'He wanted to send it to Amor or at least tell Joost he had it; and if Joost didn't stop pestering me, he would send it to Amor. It was only later, once he'd seen the video and how incriminating it actually was and had showed it to some of his friends, that he thought of blackmailing Joost. When that all turned into a disaster [she declines to explain], he got out of town, as did I. So in the end we never got a cent from it.'

Marlize is of the opinion that someone – she doesn't know who – discovered the video by accident. Apparently it was downloaded onto a laptop and no copies were made. 'Can you believe how stupid Anthony was?' she asks. 'I would have kept copies just in case.'

'In case of what?'

She doesn't elaborate. She also doesn't want to or can't explain where the laptop had been and why such a long period expired before the video surfaced. Despite the gaps in Marlize's tale, she at no time seems rehearsed or deliberately misleading.

Apparently whoever discovered the video had realised its signifi-

cance and taken it to heat *magazine. Marlize thinks it was simply to make a quick buck without having to blackmail Joost.*

Interestingly, it seems her life has never been better. Initially, when she was outed as the girl in the video and had to face up to her family and friends, she said things were awful. But now she is being offered money to appear in photo shoots and is better paid at Teazers, the strip joint where she works again (she left their employ temporarily at the time of the video). In many ways, she is a minor celebrity — unfortunately, for doing her best to ruin the life of a major celebrity.

Our deadline looms. We have 10 days in which to complete the manu-script, and all at once everything comes to a grinding halt. I am suddenly unable to arrange meetings with Joost. Obviously he knows that things are leading up to a confrontation. The time has come for him to blow my socks off.

I have worked out what I think is a Solomonesque solution to Joost's — our — dilemma. But in my heart of hearts I know it is merely a cop-out. I therefore decide to impose on not only the cleverest, but also probably the wisest person I know, my friend Constitutional Court judge Edwin Cameron. He very kindly agrees to see me and sits patiently while I explain my dilemma.

My issue is thus. I had agreed to write the book with Joost provided that it would be honest and open, and that I would not whitewash any of his indiscretions. I would not go ahead under any other circumstances. But by the same token, I didn't want to act as his judge and jury, so now, if there was a soft way out, I wanted to take it.

Once I've described my dilemma to Edwin, I give him my Solo-monesque solution. He thinks about it for a while and, I must confess, for a minute I think perhaps I haven't explained myself properly.

Then Edwin says: 'You don't really need me to tell you anything, Dave. You know the answer. But in any event, I will give you my view. Your "Solomonesque" solution, as you so eruditely describe it, is a very elegant, existential version of a confession. Unfortunately it isn't as ambiguous as you would probably like it to be, because if he was innocent you wouldn't have it in the book in the first place. So the fact that it is there means you think he is guilty. If that is the case, then it is a complete evasion of the issue.'

The problem with having really clever friends is that they understand things.

'You will simply be insulting your readers' intelligence. If you are going to confess, confess. *Don't present them with a clever-Dick explanation. It will take one intelligent reviewer and your book will be rubbished. I know you didn't want to hear this, although I equally suspect you knew it was what you were going to hear. I'm sorry, Dave, there is only one way. If he is guilty, he must confess.'*

36

The 'Solomonesque' solution or 'How I wanted to end this book'

Now that I know Joost better than I seem to know anyone else on the planet, I feel the time has come for him to blow off my socks, as originally promised. We meet at our usual haunt, Frappé, to tie up the loose ends in our opus, and I take the opportunity to confront him.

'Okay, Joost, we have reached the end of the book. After all the stuff I have read in the press, after the thousands of gratuitous opinions, after watching the video and, finally, managing to watch it right through without falling asleep, let me ask you the question I asked when we first met to do that interview: Is that you in the video?'

Joost stares at me for a while. After millions of hours spent in his company, I feel as if I'm on the brink of getting used to its unsettling effect.

'Okay, but let me first ask *you* a question,' he says. 'It's quite a long question.'

'No problem – I've got time.'

'Picture the scene. If you were in a pub – say somewhere like the Boston Tea Party in Pretoria – after being at rugby all day, where you'd been drinking ... And after more drinks in the pub you are approached for a chat by a bunch of lovely girls. And one of them happens to be unbelievably sexy, and keen, and available, and keeps letting you know that she thinks you are literally God's gift to women ... And then, after more drinks, she also makes it quite clear that she has the time and the place ...', at which point, frustratingly, he orders another black coffee.

Having placed his order, Joost looks up and says, 'Where was I?'

'At the Boston Tea Party, being attacked, so to speak, by a sexy girl ...'

He continues in that curious monotone he uses for dispensing really interesting bits of information.

'Imagine that at this point you realise you have to get home, but your mates keep bringing you ABFs ...' (A South African tradition where, before you depart, you have a series of drinks called 'Absolute Bloody Finals') '... and stupidly you keep drinking them. And because you are in one of your old stomping grounds, imagine that you keep getting a feeling of déjà vu; you keep remembering what you used to get up to and you get an irresistible urge to relive your past – just a little; just to confirm that you still have it. Then, when you think you *definitely* have to get out of there before you get into trouble, the same sexy girl reappears and repeats – although not in so many words – her offer of having some fun.' He takes a sip of his coffee.

'Lastly,' he continues, 'you have a pregnant wife and a young son at home. Let me ask you, Dave – what would you have done?'

'I know what I would have done.'

'Exactly!'

The end

It is important that I record at this point that at no stage did I discuss this ending with Joost. It was just something I hoped I could offer that would give him, in Edwin's words, an 'elegant' way out. Obviously I was being my normal naive self.

Although I may not approve of or condone anything Joost has done, I don't think it's for me to judge him one way or another. But I do feel very sorry for this extraordinary person who has been crucified so relentlessly by the press that he ended up in hospital. If there was an easier way out, I thought he should be allowed to take it; he had been punished enough.

But, alas, life is not that simple.

37

Socks time

In order to write this book in the very generous six-week deadline Zebra Press has given us, I move into my friend Mike Barnes's humble 2 000-square-metre shack.

It is truly delightful, with everything that opens and shuts and, as Mike proudly tells me, it only cost R40 million to build. The house is the flagship of one of his new developments, and for the moment stands *stoksielalleen* in a 56-hectare buck-infested park while he is waiting for subdivision rights to come through.

Below the infinity pool in front of the house is a huge dam that is home to about 25 wild ducks. Every morning, as I switch on my computer, they all religiously troop up to the pool, which is heated, and spend a couple of hours doing lengths. I often wonder what they are training for ...

The fact that it takes three days before I realise that the property has its own private helipad (and that only when Mike returns from work in his 407 Bell Helicopter) gives some indication of the size of my new abode. But, undisturbed by the outside world, it has been the perfect venue for me in which to do my work. It is also close to Joost's house, and we alternate between the shack and Frappé in Dainfern Valley.

My cellphone rings. It's Joost. 'Open up, I'm at the front door,' he says, highlighting for the umpteenth time that if you only spend R40 million on a house, you aren't guaranteed a front doorbell. I let him in. He is not looking happy.

'Can we talk?' he asks.

'Of course. What's up?'

'No, I mean can *I* talk? You shut up.'

'Okay.'

'Get your recorder. Don't say anything, don't comment and don't ask me anything. Just listen. When I'm finished, I'm leaving – please don't talk to me when I leave. Just take what I say from your recorder and put it into your good English. Don't add anything and don't remove anything.'

All very ominous.

'Are you ready?' he asks. I nod. He starts talking, at first hesitantly, and then seems to get into his stride. He continues for about five minutes and then stops, gets up, shakes my hand and leaves.

38

Joost

'In my life, I have achieved many things that took a lot of guts, determination and self-belief. I have sometimes faltered, but I have never really been scared, or doubted not making it through in the end. Perhaps that is why I actually enjoyed Kamp Staaldraad. I knew they couldn't break me.

But just when I thought life had got easier and that never again would I have to be as strong as I had been, I was confronted with something far more terrifying than anything I could ever have imagined. I came face to face with my own human frailty and my conscience. I have found that when you yourself are the problem, there is nowhere to hide. And I've tried to hide.

Throughout my life – and I suspect this also happens in everyone else's life – I have made stupid decisions. Thankfully they have usually been about inconsequential stuff that I was able to deal with by being suitably repentant or performing my own little penances. But just over three years ago I made the biggest mistake of my life. I did something I will probably regret for the rest of my days. Against all my principles, I had a sexual liaison – we never had intercourse – with a woman who was not my wife. And we took drugs. As fate would have it and unbeknown to me, the girl I was with filmed the incident.

There is not sufficient space or enough words to explain how my world came crashing down when the press reported that they had a copy of the video. I had long since blanked out the afternoon with the girl – it happened over three years ago and somehow I had hoped it would disappear into the mists of time.

The simple fact is, from almost that exact period when the

video was made, I can chart how I changed. Since then I have tried, and mostly succeeded, to live an exemplary life.

I was used to being the man who could do anything he wanted. I was *windgat* in the worst sense of the word.

I was. Until in exactly that same period Amor pulled me up – the morning I got home late after drinking with my mates at Loftus – and explained to me that I was either in our marriage or I was out. And if I was in, I had to get my act together.

Ever since, I have had 'my act' together. To then be revisited by my past so publicly was punishment so indescribably horrible that my first, and I now know incorrect, reaction was to run and hide; to deny everything and pray that for one last time in my life I could get away with my bad behaviour, because nothing like it would ever happen again. The more I denied, the more I had to deny. It just got worse and worse. My every waking moment was consumed by the video and the fact that I was living a lie.

I also asked the wrong people for advice. They promised me they could make it all go away. I had people giving me false hope that it would all be okay. I knew it couldn't possibly be okay and I fell into a spiral of self-loathing, fear, futile hope and anger that was so awful, I wouldn't wish it on my worst enemy.

Then, a few weeks ago, I ended up in hospital. Lying in bed, I knew I had to deal with the situation. So here you have my unreserved apology. No excuses. What I did with the girl was wrong. Taking drugs was wrong, and lying and denying were wrong.

More than anything, I fear losing my family. Everything else can go, but not my family. I may still lose them; I hope and pray that I don't and that Amor can find it in her heart to forgive me. To her and my other family members and all the people who believed in me, I am sorry – I let you down. Worse, still, I let myself down. I've decided to stop running and to face up to myself. I am sorry. Please forgive me.'

Joost Heystek van der Westhuizen

39

Writing Joost's book XI

When I was in my early 20s, I was spending what is now called a 'gap year' in the UK. At the time I was going through a phase of ticking off what I thought were macho challenges. So one weekend, as part of that process, a couple of mates and I found an aero club in a small town in Sussex and enrolled in a parachuting course.

We spent the Saturday afternoon in a rickety little classroom, assiduously studying the relative merits of hurling ourselves out of a perfectly airworthy aeroplane with nothing but a suspiciously worn, small piece of canvas to prevent us from smearing ourselves all over the landscape. Afterwards, in the glorious English summer's evening, we tried a bit of 'rolling' practice outside. ('Rolling', of course, as in what you do to take the shock off your feet when you land – not making joints.)

Sunday morning dawned sunny and windless, an extraordinarily perfect day for that part of the world. It wasn't long before I found myself at 3 000 feet in a noisy little Cessna with no right door. I was absolutely terrified. My Aussie instructor told me to get out and hang onto the strut to prepare for my first jump.

The actual descent was just a blur and I can hardly recall anything about it. But what I do remember is, as I landed, my girlfriend came running up and threw her arms around me. 'That was incredible,' she gushed breathlessly. 'I never knew you were so brave ...'

I couldn't help myself. I said: 'That was probably one of the most cowardly things I think I have ever done. When I climbed out of that plane onto the wheel strut, it was the scariest thing that had ever happened to me. But can you believe this? I was even more scared of asking them to bring me down in the plane and having to admit to my mates that I was too chicken to jump. And so I jumped. If I was really brave, I would have come down with the plane.'

I think Joost has spent his life being brave, doing things that any ordinary individual would have baulked at or avoided. But when something came along that he simply didn't know how to face up to, his first instinct was to run away – to deny. It can be agonisingly scary to have to face one's own imperfections.

From the moment Joost denied the truth, he was locked into a situation that grew more difficult by the day. ('Oh what a tangled web we weave, when first we practise to deceive ...') Eventually – and this is based purely on my own bubblegum psychology – his body couldn't take the strain any more, and he collapsed. In fact, Joost nearly died. If his visitor hadn't been able to administer CPR, he would almost certainly not have been alive today.

For him to then confess to his transgressions when, in all likelihood, he would rather have rested and fully recovered must rank as one of the hardest things he has done in his life.

The way ahead is not going to be easy for Joost, but at least he has finally faced his demons. For me, that fact alone proves he has the courage to deal with whatever slings and arrows outrageous fortune hurls at him. He will survive, because, in the end, Joost van der Westhuizen has chosen to come down with the plane.

PS. *These last few months I have really enjoyed delving into who the real Joost van der Westhuizen is, and hopefully he will stay my NBF. Who knows, when I eventually get used to his glare, uh ... stare, I might even one day drop the N ...*

PPS. *... and I have to admit, without a shadow of a doubt, he has completely blown my socks off.*

Epilogue

It's a typical, bitterly cold winter's morning. Joost walks in looking as if he has just been put through a mangle. He is very pale and his eyes are red. He doesn't look as if he has slept.

'I told Amor last night ...'

'And ...?'

'She was very angry; in fact, she *is* furious ...'

'What did you expect her to do, congratulate you?'

He ignores me and sits down. 'Then I went and told my mother.'

'What did she say?'

'Nothing but support, support, support; she was amazing.'

'She's your mother. Tell me, is there anything you can think of that Jordan or Kylie could do to make you hate them?'

'Of course not,' he says without hesitation. 'My dad is also incredible. How he is always there when I need him.'

'Parents love their kids regardless, unconditionally. I don't think any of us appreciate our folks until we get into trouble.'

There's a long silence, then he asks tiredly, 'What's going to happen when the book comes out?'

'I think there will probably be a small fuss. I also think you are going to get a lot of flak. People are very angry with you. Hopefully, once everybody's had their say, they will leave you alone. Maybe you should borrow one of Mike's crash helmets and hire a suit of armour? I don't think it is going to be easy. But one thing is indisputable – you have finally done the right thing. No one can take that away from you.'

There is another silence.

Then the Springbok legend responds: 'It's chilly this morning. Aren't you cold in here?' He stares blankly down towards the floor for a moment.

'*Fok, Engelsman, jy dra nie eers kouse nie!*' — you're not even wearing socks!

Afterword

I met David Gemmell, the author of *Joost: The Man in the Mirror*, while in Pretoria assisting Springbok assistant coach Dick Muir with his inaugural International Rugby Academy. David mentioned to me during a short interview that he was nearing completion of Joost's biography and how Joost had admired me from a distance. To my amazement, David said that Joost would be honoured if I would write the Afterword to his book. My first thought was, I hardly know the guy and probably haven't broken bread with him for well over a decade, so what the hell am I going to write? Having read a good portion of the book and learnt of the controversial events in recent months of Joost's life, I am delighted to have been given the honour of writing these few words.

I share with Joost the privilege of playing in a Rugby World Cup–winning team and every special memory that goes with that. But our 1991 victory perhaps was a little hollow in that it was the last time the Springboks would be excluded from the event. That said, they did return to the international fold the following year, and I had the enormous satisfaction of leading my team in a one-off test at Newlands in August 1992. The next year I would play my last three tests against the Boks in Australia. Robert du Preez would be my scrumhalf opponent in those tests, but in a match between tests playing for the NSW Waratahs at Concord Oval in Sydney I came up against a tough and somewhat arrogant yet very skilful youngster, one Joost van der Westhuizen.

Soon after retirement I disappeared to France to join a French investment bank. The rugby umbilical cord was largely cut as I started a new career in a foreign land. Then in May of 1995, with television commentary commitments for the Rugby World Cup, I returned to South Africa for the duration of the tournament. Of the seven World Cups played to date, it is my view that the 1995 event was the most memorable for all the right reasons, namely the Mandela factor and the emergence of this amazing team that bonded a nation that seemed divided when I first led my team there in 1992. Back then black and coloured people would come up to me wishing my team would stuff the Boks. The '95 World Cup was different – the Rainbow Nation rallied around this team and hope seemed to emerge for a future united by the team's perseverance and ultimate triumph.

Right at the belly button of this unfolding success in '95 was the kid who spoke the foreign language and had got in my face back in 1993 in Sydney. Van der Westhuizen had emerged as a dominant player with all the scrumhalf attributes: a long quick pass, a strong running and kicking game, lateral vision, great defence and ultimately a will to do whatever it would take to succeed. He was not going to die wondering and, when I reflect on the '95 tournament, nor were his teammates or management. It was simply damn the torpedoes full speed ahead.

From a distance I admired Joost's ongoing rugby career and scrumhalf dominance as the game launched into the professional era. But, as I have stated, I never really got to meet the man or share with him what the French term the 'third half' – the times away from the playing pitch where real friendships are harnessed over a beer. Quite simply, our playing careers never really over-lapped and upon retirement I moved on from the game.

I was fascinated while writing this Afterword to read a little about Joost's early days on the farm – to learn what life in South Africa during the apartheid years was like for a young Afrikaans boy and to see his passion for sport and rugby as I recalled my own childhood and the similarities. I was also interested to read how, in one match in 1998 after winning the Currie Cup, Joost believed the success was God's will. Obviously a spiritual man, a man of prayer, again I saw the similarities between us.

Which brings me to the recent controversy in 2009. Here in Australia we heard little of the supposed incident with the young lady. But I gather that in South Africa it dominated the press and became an enormous scandal as it was played out very publicly. I have been privy to David Gemmell's writings on the topic and also to Joost's own admissions after original denials of the events of that fateful day. My faith and understanding of the gospel have me believe that God sent his Son because of a problem He had with mankind. Quite simply, we bugger things up from time to time and our unrighteousness breaks the relationship between man and God. Christ through his shedding of blood restores that relationship if we believe in Him. Every reader of this book will know of many times they have fallen short, made dumb decisions, wished they had never ventured down that road. I could fill this book with my own shortcomings.

Joost made a bad error of judgement. I hope he has been forgiven by those closest to him. I personally trust that, as his children grow up and in years to come read this biography, they will know that, like them, Dad is not perfect. I hope that they will be hugely proud to say that Joost van der Westhuizen is their dad and give thanks for everything he has achieved and will continue to achieve.

Nick Farr-Jones
Former Wallaby captain

The Guy in the Glass

When you get what you want in your struggle for pelf,
And the world makes you King for a day,
Then go to the mirror and look at yourself,
And see what that guy has to say.

For it isn't your Father, or Mother, or Wife,
Who judgement upon you must pass.
The feller whose verdict counts most in your life
Is the guy staring back from the glass.

He's the feller to please, never mind all the rest,
For he's with you clear up to the end,
And you've passed your most dangerous, difficult test
If the guy in the glass is your friend.

You may be like Jack Horner and 'chisel' a plum,
And think you're a wonderful guy,
But the man in the glass says you're only a bum
If you can't look him straight in the eye.

You can fool the whole world down the pathway of years,
And get pats on the back as you pass,
But your final reward will be heartaches and tears
If you've cheated the guy in the glass.

— DALE WIMBROW

Glossary

bossies: mad, crazy
Fok, manne: Fuck, guys
Is jy nou klaar gepraat?: Have you finished talking?
kaffir: highly derogatory term for black person
kak-makers: shit-stirrers
klap: smack
Kom manne: Come guys
mal: mad, crazy
oupa: grandpa
Pa, ek wil sulke skoene hê, asseblief: Dad, I would like shoes like those, please
platsak: broke
skelm: underhand
sommer: because
spook: ghost
stoksielalleen: alone
Waar gaan jy?: Where are you going?
Wat gaan aan?: What's happening?

Do you have any comments, suggestions or
feedback about this book or any other Zebra Press titles?
Contact us at **talkback@zebrapress.co.za**